Changing Behavior

Immediately Transform Your Relationships with Easy-to-Learn, Proven Communication Skills

Patent Pending on Model of
Behavioral Engagement and Pure Presence™

ISBN -13: 978-1517001292
ISBN -10: 1517001293
Library of Congress Control Number: 2011938210
NIWH, Boston, Massachusetts
Published by SoulWork Press, Boston

For my children, Kimberly, Conor, and Ryan,
who make everything worthwhile,
and for Brian, always

TABLE OF CONTENTS

Foreword

If someone said you could transform your life and enhance your relationships by using a few simple communication techniques that can be applied in almost any setting, wouldn't you want to do that? Wouldn't you want to learn those skills? If the answer is yes, you've picked up the right book. This is an easy-to-read guide that is loaded with simple skills that have been scientifically shown to have a huge impact on your relationships!

When asked to write a few words about my experience of learning and applying Behavior Engagement™, I was honored and delighted to do so. Dr. Georgianna Donadio's years of experience in nursing, hospital administration, and health care practice, along with her passion for transforming lives through Whole Health Education®, has really resonated with me and has been an inspiration to integrate this same philosophy into my own career.

Over the past many years as a nurse and hospital administrator myself, I have seen amazing advances in medical technology and diagnostics. Yet chronic illness and disease are still on the rise. I believe Dr. Donadio's research addresses a critical component missing from our health care delivery system: engaging the whole person in a self-directed healing process and providing them with the knowledge and skills they need for lifelong health and wellness.

Behavioral Engagement is different from other behavioral change models in that it respects and honors all aspects of the whole person—their beliefs, feelings, thoughts, and values—as well as what each person innately knows is right for them. Behavioral Engagement offers a simple set of skills and tools that can be applied in a variety of settings, both clinical and personal.

These skills and tools have a dramatic effect on relationships with family, friends, and colleagues, and they can facilitate *sustainable* behavioral change. I know because I have personally had the opportunity to learn these skills from Dr. Donadio and have witnessed the results.

When applying the process of Behavioral Engagement in my own life, I have experienced many positive effects. As Georgianna describes, it all starts with being open to the process, clearing yourself of any preconceived ideas about the dialogue to come, and engaging in the conversation with the intent of applying the skills to be purely present to another person.

As a mother and wife, I have been amazed to see how this process has strengthened my relationship with my family and allowed for a complete connection, an easing of difficult discussions, a clearer understanding, and the creation of stronger relationships. As an administrator, I have seen difficult conversations becoming easier, and have even seen improvements in job satisfaction along with improvements in well-being. Now, who can argue with that?

The model is truly amazing. Based upon Dr. Donadio's pioneering and innovative research, creating an environment that is centered on the communication skills of respectful and mindful listening, complete openness, and Pure Presence can really change whatever environment you are in.

Deeply connecting with another person and being present with your whole self in a way that allows them to connect with their own inner knowledge and wisdom is what Behavioral Engagement is all about. By using the skills outlined in this book, which are both scientifically grounded and have been tested in a number of clinical settings, you will enhance your life and the lives of others around you.

I'm not saying this is easy, but if you have the intention to practice and apply the skills, it will become a natural part of who you are. If you want to transform your life and see dramatic effects in the relationships around you, this book is for you.

Thank you, Georgianna, for the passion you have demonstrated in creating a program that can offer such a transformation in our lives, as well as the world around us. And, congratulations to all who learn and apply the skills from this wonderful and compelling book!

Beth Borg, RN, MHA
Clinical Operations Administrator, Mayo Clinic

"We can't solve problems by using the same kind of thinking
we used when we created them."
—Albert Einstein

A New Tool for Transforming Relationships

As an educator, I have a deep appreciation and profound respect for the potential of the union of knowledge and compassion to bring about change and eliminate conflict. The expression that *knowledge is power* is truly poignant. Knowledge can re-inform our beliefs and worldview, which in turn can allow us to shift our perceptions and behaviors. Compassion enables us to live more meaningful lives and achieve connections.

This book is the result of a unique health education and behavioral change program that was originally created to re-educate health care professionals in how they can more effectively demystify health information and communicate with their patients. The same hospital-tested relationship, communication, and behavioral change skills taught to the doctors and nurses are shared here for you to enhance and enrich your own personal relationships.

We start the discussion of behavioral change with an examination of the *challenge of being human.* This is a complex subject and one that is intertwined with our need for relationships, as well as our need to understand and resolve the conflicts that arise within them.

Part I presents the origins of behavior and the importance of relationships, then *cuts right to the chase* with a step-by-step "how to" chapter on applying Behavioral Engagement™, the behavioral change model developed and researched for more than thirty years in Boston hospitals and in medical centers around the country.

Part II provides a comprehensive look at behaviors and culture in the United States as well as addresses the statistics and data on our current health and relationship behaviors.

As you move through the book, it may feel like you are taking a course or training in relationship communications, and in a sense, you are. The information contained in these chapters will provide a new understanding of the challenges we deal with each day in our relationships, as well as easy-to-learn, proven communication skills for transforming those relationships.

There are personal inquiry questions at the end of the chapters that invite you to think about the information you have read and how it might be applicable to your own relationships. It can be helpful to think of this book as a *continuing education program*, which is exactly what it is for our health professionals, who receive continuing education credit hours for their studies.

It would not be a bad idea if we were all required to take continuing education courses in relationships, just as professionals are required to do in their area of expertise or practice. As *National Geographic* writer and explorer Dan Buettner, who traveled the globe in search of answers on longevity and happiness, said in his 2010 interview on National Public Radio, *"Relationships are really the key to lifelong happiness."*

Relationships are an important part of our lives, and the more knowledge and skills we have to apply to them, the better relationships we can develop. Positive relationships benefit all of us.

With all good wishes,
Georgianna

Changing Behavior

PART I

Chapter One
The Challenge of Being Human

"People are itchy and lost and bored and quick to jump to any fix. Why is there such a vast self-help industry in this country? Why do all these selves need help? They have been deprived of something by our psychological culture. They have been deprived of the sense that there is something else in life, some purpose that has come with them into the world."
—James Hillman, PhD
Little Acorns: A Radical New Psychology

We all want to be valued. And in the deepest part of ourselves, we know that. Yet it is forgotten when we encounter each other. What we then do is revert to the *pecking order* impulse and size up another person to establish either their comparative worth to us or our superiority to them, forgetting that each of us wears an invisible sign that reads, *"Notice me; make me feel important."*

We also forget this in our intimate relationships when our need to be valued can overshadow everything else. Many of us are unfulfilled in our lives, and many of us have *hungry hearts*. There is a way to change this and create healthy, fulfilling relationships, but most of us do not know how. Instead we continue to behave as we always have and continue to experience the same outcomes.

What we want in our relationships is for another person to listen, with genuine interest, to our story, our suffering, our hopes, and our dreams. We want them to care about our life—and not because of some self-serving agenda on their part. Being present to another person in a fully engaged and authentic way connects us with our true *self* as well as connects us with the other person. Being *purely present* to another person, or they with us, is a deeply fulfilling experience.

Our relationships give us emotional nourishment and can be the spark that motivates and inspires us to live more authentically, to re-direct and re-shape ourselves in a new and joyful way. To repeat Dan Buettner's earlier comment, *"Relationships are really the key to lifelong happiness."*[1] We want them, we need them, and we continually seek them.

Having the right skills to create healthy, thriving relationships is important. How to create these types of relationships is not something we are taught to do. We learn about relationships with our eyes and ears from observing our family members, our peers, and surrounding environment. Unfortunately for many of us, the skills we have learned do not result in successful and healthy relationships.

It is now well established that our relationships are intimately connected to our state of health. Experiencing the pain of repeated failed relationships can deeply undermine our well-being and self-confidence and lead to loneliness, depression, and chronic illness. Knowing this, it makes good sense to learn relational skills that can help us create more positive and successful outcomes.

By having a better understanding of why we behave as we do, and by learning new skills and knowledge that can facilitate the transformation of our behaviors and thus our relationships, we will improve our relational outcomes as well as the overall state of our health and well-being.

Changing behavior is not easy. The way we behave and why we behave as we do is as unique to each of us as our fingerprints or DNA. Although changing our behavior is challenging, the rewards can be enormous. By changing our relational behaviors we can re-direct all aspects of our life—enhancing our happiness, our work, and our personal fulfillment, and even increasing our longevity.

It's Complicated

To be a human being is a complex and challenging experience. We have basic physical, emotional, social, nutritional, environmental, and spiritual needs that require attention on a regular basis. We also have instincts, thoughts, feelings, beliefs, and impulses that interact with these basic needs. Collectively, they all influence how we view and experience the world around us. These multifaceted and compelling needs are unique for each of us and are the prime movers of our behavior.

To develop the skills and behaviors necessary to create the type of relationships we desire, we need to start with an understanding of how these basic survival needs are integrated with brain functions that produce various kinds of behaviors. To understand how these aspects of ourselves are developed and connected to each other, let's take a quick look at where and how behaviors originate in the brain and nervous system.

Where *Do* Behaviors Come From?

Specifically, how do we learn to behave the way we do and why are our behaviors so persistent? These are age-old questions asked and partially answered by many who are tasked with addressing the topic. Psychologists, educators, scientists, and others have pondered and researched the topic of human behavior for decades. The current understanding of where behavior starts is at the primary site of development—in our central nervous system—with the perception of pain and pleasure.

This pleasure-pain perception is critically important to human survival as an adaptation mechanism that can be identified as early as the third trimester of pregnancy, when the specialized *thalamocortical* neuron connections in the brain are developing within the fetus.[2] The pleasure-pain perception allows us to respond to our environment by either moving away from what feels painful or moving toward what feels pleasurable. We will soon see just how important this mechanism is in connection with how we behave, as well as how this primal drive in human beings influences and informs our behaviors in relationships.

The Pleasure-Pain Principle

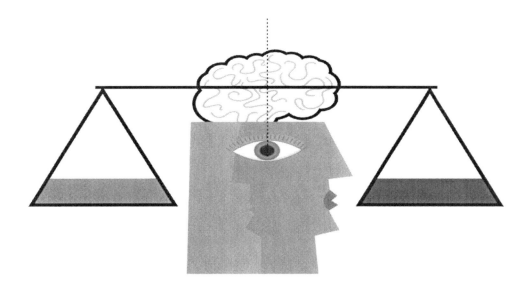

Freud's well-known *Pleasure-Pain Principle* says that people seek pleasure and avoid pain. Jeremy Bentham's classic *Principles of Morals and Legislation* found pleasure and pain to be *"the sole motivators and the only absolutes in this world."*[3] The principles are based on deeply embedded neurological mechanisms that help explain why it is so difficult to achieve sustainable behavioral change.

Situations or experiences that *threaten our perception* of personal survival are associated with pain and fear. Situations or experiences that *enhance our perception* of personal survival are associated with pleasure and the absence of fear. An example is the potential self-abuse associated with excessive eating, smoking, and drug and alcohol use. Although we can intellectually understand the potential health risks associated with such behaviors, the attachment to or avoidance of these excesses is greatly influenced by our conscious and often unconscious perception of their ability to produce either pleasure or pain.

The fear or anticipation of pain is often the major deterrent to making health-behavior or relationship-behavior changes. Even when behaving in a particular way leads to conflict, or the loss of a relationship, we will make only those behavioral changes that are within our pleasure-pain comfort zone.

Pleasure-Pain Imprints

When we first enter the world, our nervous system and brain are like a new computer with no data stored on its neurological hard drive. The process of placing data into this developing *computer-brain* occurs with sensory-motor input that comes from our immediate external environment.

The five senses of sight, sound, smell, taste, and touch communicate information from the surrounding environment to the brain, which in turn determines if we are safe or in danger, and if it is necessary to respond or adapt to survive. These sensory-motor recordings from birth to age five are deeply formative and persistent.

If, as a small child, we are bitten by a dog or stung by a bee, the sensory-motor pain-fear data that is sent to our brain when we experience the event is recorded in the neurological database. This becomes permanent information that the brain will identify as painful or potentially threatening to our survival. Even a *perceived* threat can trigger pleasure-pain memory and the fear that can accompany it.

How Survival Adaptation Works

The human sensory-motor communication system is the primal survival adaptation mechanism commonly known as the "fight or flight" response, which has developed over millions of years of evolution. The good news is that this remarkable mechanism, which allows us to discern and escape from danger, is what has saved us from becoming an extinct species.

The bad news, however, is that this same ability to enhance survival is also the basis of our emotional and instinctual behaviors. This "fight or flight" system, rooted in survival adaptation, can become a self-limiting and ironically a self-destructive responder to stimuli that is only *perceived* as threatening.

We will see the importance of understanding this most basic human reaction to the various types of stimuli in our lives and how this reaction can create the difficulty many individuals experience in making sustainable behavioral changes in the areas of their relationships, their health, and their habits, as well as in how they communicate with others.

Where It Begins

By the time we are seven or eight years of age, billions of sensory motor stimuli and messages have informed us how to respond and adapt to our environment in order to provide the best possible chance of survival. The rudimentary brain and nervous system are the first to develop in the fetus at approximately twenty-one to twenty-eight days after conception. The nervous system is essential for all communication to take place between ourselves and the environment we are in. We can only *feel*, experience, and interact with our world through this remarkable mechanism that is connected to every cell in our body.

From these neurological feelings or responses come our protective strategies of how to live and survive, what to believe and value, and ultimately, how we form our worldview. These psychological perceptions are drawn from what we experience within the environment we are raised in. Our environment is both external and internal, made up of incoming stimuli from outside the self, and internal stimuli—biochemical or physiological—that send messages to our brain. These developed adaptation patterns become integrated with *personality* and have a significant effect on our behavior.

They can create successful strategies or problematic behaviors. Finding successful, sustainable ways to move beyond problematic behaviors is the focus of all behavioral change models. One important component to this neurological adaptation is each individual's level of resilience. Resilience, the ability to adapt, is what distinguishes those of us who thrive from those who "fail to thrive."

Resilience develops through genetics and environmental conditioning. Today, it is well documented that resilience is an important factor in how well we survive or are able to adapt to stressful environments. Much behavioral change research is currently focused on understanding the mechanisms of resilience and how we can foster this important conditioning. To better understand the challenge of behavioral change let's take a quick look at our fascinating and amazing brain.

How the Brain Is Wired, Made Easy

The Brain Stem

The human brain has evolved to a multi-compartmentalized structure from what is referred to as the *reptilian brain*, believed to be more than 500 million years old. This primitive neurological structure is the oldest part of the brain. It is also known as the *autonomic* or automatic component, as it is responsible for vital life support functions such as breathing, heart rate, blood pressure, and so forth.

This is the *coma* brain, which keeps our bodily organs functioning without benefit of the thought process. This part of the brain *thinks* in a different way from how the intellectual brain does, and it is this specialized *thinking* or interpreting of the sensory-motor information from the environment that is critical to our individual survival. The brain stem is the conduit for all sensory-motor information to and from the brain, as well as the conduit for all nerves that exit and enter the skull and body. This part of the brain is primarily involved in communicating incoming data to the thinking portion of the brain.

The brain stem could be called the *stimuli gatekeeper,* as it plays the important role of regulating the central nervous system. All sensations going to the brain and signals coming from the brain to the muscles must pass through the brain stem. Brain-stem injuries are a serious threat to survival, as this critical part of our neurological wiring affects all other parts of the brain and the body as well.

The Midbrain and the Amazing Amygdala

The midbrain is believed to be between 200 and 300 million years old. Because this brain structure is highly developed in mammals, it is referred to as the *mammalian* brain. It is strongly involved with emotional reactions related to survival and contains the amygdala. The amygdala is a highly sensitive arousal system that responds to sensory motor input and stimuli. The amygdala is often referred to as the *center of emotions.*

Visual (sight), auditory (sound), olfactory (smell), gustatory (taste), and somato-sensory (touch) stimulate this complex structure to produce a wide range of behavioral functions. It is widely connected to multiple parts of the brain and communicates reactions and various arousal responses and behaviors. The midbrain is considered the *emotional gatekeeper*.

The midbrain is affected by both neurological and hormonal stimulation. The adrenal hormone epinephrine, pituitary hormone regulator dopamine, nervous system neurotransmitter acetylcholine, and nerve impulse neurotransmitter serotonin act upon the amygdala to communicate physiological and psychological information important to individual survival. It is easy to understand why the amygdala is currently one of the most heavily researched and studied brain areas.

The Forebrain

The forebrain is the *newest* part of the human brain. Our modern cortex is believed to be a mere 100,000 years old. It is the site of our intelligence, memory, personality, speech, and ability to move and feel. It contains the cerebrum, which could be thought of as the *gatekeeper of our thoughts*.

Our brains, like computers, become programmed by data input. This input informs us of our environment so we may react and behave accordingly—away from pain and toward pleasure. We respond positively to reward (pleasure) and negatively to punishment (pain).

Understanding the complexity, and at the same time the simplicity, of *brain function–nervous system–survival adaptation* helps us become more patient with and compassionate about our own behaviors. This understanding also translates into a greater patience with and acceptance of the behaviors of others.

As we become more aware of brain functions and the pleasure-pain mechanism, we can see why our behaviors may be more complex than we imagined. Many of us believe it is a matter of identifying a strategy to solve a problem and then implementing that strategy. Rational, cognitive approaches to behavioral change can provide structure and tools to work with. However, when it comes to making sustainable changes, emotions trump cognitive thoughts hands down.

Beliefs, Emotions, and Worldview

Emotions, beliefs, and worldview play a large role in our behavioral choices. Merriam-Webster Online defines *emotions, beliefs,* and *worldview* as follows:

> Emotion—a conscious mental reaction (as anger or fear) subjectively experienced as strong feeling usually directed toward a specific object and typically accompanied by physiological and behavioral changes in the body

> Beliefs—conviction of the truth of some statement or the reality of some being or phenomenon especially when based on examination of evidence

> Worldview—a particular philosophy of life or conception of the world.

These three components of the *self* strongly influence our behavioral choices as well as our attachment to those choices. New research out of the University of Michigan suggests that we base our opinions on our emotions, beliefs, and worldview and that when presented with contradictory facts, we adhere even more strongly to our original beliefs, which are rooted in our emotions.[4]

One would logically assume that factual evidence should clarify and influence a person's choices or their acceptance of, for instance, a political candidate or someone they know or their family members and so forth. Rather, the study shows that people *dig their heels in more deeply* and resist changing any of their beliefs, emotions, or views even when confronted with undeniable, overwhelming proof that runs against their position. This is another example of how our emotions and attachments to our beliefs and worldview influence our behavior more than intellectual thinking, rational judgment, or pragmatic reasoning.

Feeling and Thinking

Thinking does not change behavior. If it did, it would be easy for any of us to think we need to lose a few pounds and have our intellectual-thinking brain direct our body to make the behavioral changes necessary to bring about the weight loss. That is not to say that many individuals cannot do this for short periods of time, because we can and do lose weight or stop smoking for short intervals. Then, the majority of the time, what derails this desired change is a new stimulus of threat or fear that reactivates the stored data or unconscious memory of an event, as well as our personalized response to that data or memory.

This triggered *pleasure-pain* experience often returns us to behaviors—such as smoking, overeating, excessive drinking, or other self-soothing behaviors—we have just spent much time and effort to eliminate. This triggering is an emotional response to the perceived threat (pain) or fear. We often attempt to eliminate this fear through any number of self-soothing behaviors that will produce chemical reactions in the body that are intended to help reduce the anxiety.

At the Beckman Institute for Advanced Science and Technology at the University of Illinois at Urbana–Champaign, cognitive neuroscientists are researching and investigating emotional functioning—how interactions between various regions of the brain relate to mood, and the link between the mental process of *knowing* and our emotions.[5]

This is an exciting and fascinating area of research that will one day help us better understand how to address the emotional triggering that so often derails positive change. What is clear at this point about emotions is that this *feeling* component of our brain function is intimately and more powerfully linked to our behaviors than our knowing- or thinking-brain component.

Nature Versus Nurture

Although there are numerous theories relating to the origin and function of emotions, two of the most examined are evolutionary psychology, which views emotions as *adaptations* representing the *human psychological nature,* and the oldest but less favored nineteenth-century theory by scholars William James and Carl Lange. Known as the James-Lange theory on the origins of emotions, it says that *"emotions are feelings resulting from physiological changes."*[6]

These two theories represent the classic *nature* (James-Lange theory) versus *nurture* (evolutionary psychology) debate. However, although there is currently no scientific certainty of exactly where in the mind or the body the physical sensation of emotion is experienced, the work of Klaus Scherer provides an excellent definition of the *function* of emotions.

Scherer says that *"the principal design and function of emotion in humans is to mediate relationships. Events which are the focus of emotions are predominately social. They connect primarily with others; those with whom we have conflict; those with whom we are attached and those with whom we love."*[7]

The James-Lange theory attributes emotions to physiology. We see that even within the womb, we are conditioned or nurtured by the hormonal, nutritional, emotional, social, and physical environment within which we are formed. Our personality, and the way we act in different situations, is also a form of adaptation—both physically and mentally. Often, individuals who did not experience a balanced or healthy upbringing may suffer from the pain of feeling they are not valued or worthy of love, or from a fear of inadequacy. They will adopt behaviors that both deny their fear or pain and create a means to elicit the pleasure and approval they need.

They may mask their feelings with such behaviors as being *the life of the party*, a great person to have a good time with, funny, charming, or easy to get along with. In actuality, their outgoing, superficial behavior is a protective adaptation to insulate them from re-experiencing the early fear of inadequacy, feelings of unworthiness, or risk of rejection through their attempt to please everyone they meet and have everyone like them.

This type of adaptation can be a successful coping strategy that produces pleasure and avoids pain. It can also prevent emotional intimacy. These are difficult behaviors to change. The pain-pleasure-reward-punishment conditioning of a prior psychological trauma, and the resulting adaptive behaviors to self-sooth the trauma, are anchored in the unconscious, survival-driven brain.

Psychology and the study of human behavior is a vast science that explores why particular experiences produce particular behaviors. There are many theories and models of therapy that offer interesting and complex explanations for human behavior. Yet the one constant in our behavioral motivation is our *primal pleasure-pain drive*. Unless we have developed an unhealthy pleasure in experiencing pain, we will always avoid it and move toward the sensation of pleasure. The unique stimuli our brain and nervous system receive define what our experience of pain or pleasure is. This pleasure-pain conditioning has a significant impact on adaptation behaviors and drives many of our relationship behaviors.

Our behavioral choices express how we have uniquely crafted our individual survival adaptations to avoid pain and pursue pleasure. The longer we live with these adaptations or behaviors, the more difficult it becomes to change them.

The Behavior of Others

Most of us are well aware of how behaviors can create both pleasure and fulfillment or dissatisfaction and conflict. Trying to resolve conflict and the desire to understand others in addition to having our own needs met are two compelling aspects of human relationships. Have you ever caught pieces of someone's conversation on a cell phone or gathered with coworkers around the water cooler?

Once the pleasantries are out of the way, what is generally the most common topic of discussion? It is about relationships and specifically about the *behavior of others* in those relationships. Rarely do we discuss our own behavior as a problem. It is usually the behavior of others we are concerned with.

If we are candid, most of us will remember those times in a relationship when, after the *honeymoon* period was over, we tried to make the other person change his or her behavior—especially once we saw their behaviors as flawed or not reflecting the feelings or appreciation we desire in a partner.

In his *Psychology Today* magazine column, psychologist Steven Stosny, PhD, talks about what couples are really arguing about in relationships:

[Cohabitating] couples don't fight about what they think they fight about. It's not "the big [issues]" they identify in surveys: money, sex, kids, or house-work. ... Lovers fight when they believe their partners don't care about how they feel. They fight about the pain of disconnection.[8]

Most of our behaviors, as Stosny points out, are generated by our primal mechanism of wanting to be cared for and valued. As we explore human behavior in the upcoming chapters, consider how the underlying messages of our behavior in relationships stem from this primal mechanism. We don't stop and think, "How am I reacting to what she said?" or "Why am I behaving this way?" We react to the situation emotionally, *not* intellectually.

Health and Behavior

In November 1996, a fifteen-year study by the Harvard School of Public Health was published that showed that up to 70% of all chronic disease is generated by our behaviors.[9] Smoking, overeating, lack of exercise, and excessive use of alcohol are the leading contributors to heart disease, obesity, high blood pressure, type 2 diabetes, cancer, and stroke.

Many of us know that our lifestyle and health behaviors lead to the chronic conditions we suffer from, yet we cannot seem to change them. The same thing is true for our relationships. It appears that our survival adaptation behaviors for avoiding pain and seeking pleasure are so deeply embedded in us that, ironically, we avoid change to the point of endangering our lives.

Harvard psychology professor Robert Kegan, PhD, the William and Miriam Meehan Professor in Adult Learning, cites a recent study that concluded, *"Doctors can tell heart patients that they will literally die if they do not change their ways, and still only one in seven will be able to make the changes. They want to live out their lives, fulfill their dreams and watch their grandchildren grow up. These are not people who want to die. And, still they cannot make the changes they need in order to survive."*[10]

This study raises the obvious question of what makes changing the way we live such a daunting and difficult task and why we have not yet found definitive answers and solutions for it.

Changing Health Behaviors

In health care, the exploration of behavioral change models is ongoing. As the cost of providing health care services continue to increase, along with our rapidly expanding chronic-care population, finding alternatives that can reduce the need for health care services is desirable.

Over the last twenty years, the application of behavior modification and disease management models has not been successful in improving statistical outcomes or creating sustainable health-behavior change. A current and well-used health-behavior change program is the Stages of Change model developed by James Prochaska, PhD, of the University of Rhode Island, and his research colleagues.

This six-stage change model has been shown to be effective in identifying the *staging* for when behavioral change occurs and has identified ways to encourage health-behavior change in those stages.[11]

In clinical studies in 2002,[12] 2004,[13] and 2007,[14] this model demonstrated initial improvement to preliminary health-behavior change. However, like the Behavior Modification and Disease Management models previously used, this program did not identify tools that produced long periods of sustainability once the patient moved into the *action* and *maintenance* stages of the model.

Prochaska acknowledges the complexity and challenge of making behavioral change and the greater challenge in achieving sustained change in *Changing for Good*, a book he co-authored:

In fact, it can be argued that all change is self change. This [changing behavior] is tough work, but nothing else will do. For example, although many diets succeed in the short term, their long term success is quite low. Many dieters lose weight quickly, but six months after beginning a diet, many people weigh more than they did when they started.[15]

Getting Our Attention

Just as in health-behavior change, it often takes a painful or threatening event of such severity that we begin to pay attention to the other person's needs within the relationship. The threat of a relationship breakup or divorce can be so painful or upsetting that we want to *do* something about *fixing* it.

Despite the struggles of relationships and raising children, we are willing to work hard at making relationships last, because for most of us they hold great importance and meaning in our lives. Martin Seligman, PhD, the father of positive psychology, says, *"If we just wanted positive emotions, our species would have died out a long time ago. Why [do] couples go on having children even though the data clearly shows that parents are less happy than childless couples?*

Why [do] billionaires desperately seek more money even when there was nothing they wanted to do with it? We have children to pursue other elements of well-being. We want meaning in life. We want relationships."[16]

Many of us have learned that even when our primary relationship is at its all-time low, staying in it can be preferable to our leaving or the other person leaving the relationship. Even if we say we are staying because of finances, practical considerations, or because we do not want to leave the children, we stay with the hope of making the relationship better because the pain of *losing love*—either through the death of a relationship or the actual death of a loved one—is one of the most intense pains a human being can experience. We can feel more threatened by the possibility of losing an intimate relationship than by receiving a serious medical diagnosis. Often we are more willing to work on improving a relationship than work on improving our health issues.

It may seem counterintuitive that many of us would rather pay attention to saving a relationship than to saving our own life—ensuring our survival—which is the primary human drive. Why is this so? Because many of us will go into denial after receiving a serious medical diagnosis, whereas the threat of losing love, or an intimate relationship, as Seligman points out, is about *emotional disconnection*—a more immediate type of death. This threat of disconnection can motivate us to quickly do something to eliminate that threat, like change our behavior, because as Freud identified, *"We are never as hopelessly unhappy as when we lose love."*

Let's Look at a New Model of Behavioral Change

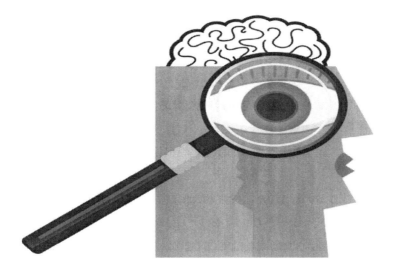

Since 1980, the National Institute of Whole Health has been developing and testing a model of behavioral change called Behavioral Engagement™ with *Pure Presence*. Although this model was developed for application in health care settings, it applies to all types of relationships. Human beings come to relationships with the same needs. These needs are generally not focused on in the day-to-day unfolding of a relationship.

Decades of pilot studies and research have shown that when applied to relationships, Behavioral Engagement (BE) can facilitate deeply satisfying communication and relational changes. However, it requires a clear understanding of the mechanisms at work within the model, and, most important, understanding that BE is not about changing someone else's behavior. Rather, it is about changing our own behavior, which invites the other person to make changes from their own self-directed desire to do so.

When behaviors are invited to evolve through the experience of being purely present with another person, and not because we wish to please someone or be a compliant patient or codependent partner, even the most resistant individuals can and do change their behaviors. What is required is the absence of subtextual or obvious intent of someone wanting the individual to change.

What the Research Demonstrated

The pilot studies the institute conducted in developing and testing the Behavioral Engagement model contain countless stories of individuals who were completely unwilling to make any behavioral changes even though they were *"one emergency room admission away from the undertaker,"* as one of the referring physicians commented. The physician who was the primary investigator of one of the pilot studies told the BE providers that he *"stacked the deck"* against the study by recruiting the most ill and behaviorally challenged individuals possible.

One memorable story is told by a physician who referred one of his patients to the study. The doctor did not believe this particular person would make any changes in an effort to save his own life, because he had repeatedly refused to do so in the past. The man had serious heart disease and diabetes, smoked, and drank alcohol even though these behaviors were exacerbating his conditions; he was chronically ill, physically stooped over, had an unhealthy pallor, and regularly presented a negative disposition.

About twelve weeks after that patient began participating in the study, the referring physician was walking down the hall in the hospital and heard someone calling after him. He turned to see whom it was but could not identify the man speaking to him. When the man identified himself, the physician could not believe this was the same stooped-over, negative, uncooperative individual he had referred into the study. Before him stood that same man, standing upright, looking healthier, and, even more surprising, appearing hopeful. Here was someone who had obviously changed his attitude, his weight, and his overall appearance. Here was a person who *"had been re-moralized with renewed interest in health and well-being."*[17]

The BE facilitator shared with the physician, as well as the other facilitators, the story of her experience with this particular individual. At first, he was completely resistant to working with her and did not trust that she was not going to try to *"do"* something to him. He told her that the only reason he was going to *"stick around"* was that he wanted to find out *"what she was selling."*

On the last day the facilitator worked with this patient, the man turned to her and said, *"By the way, I figured out what you've been selling—you've been selling me to me!"*

In other words, *"You valued and respected me and demonstrated to me that my feelings and insights and what I know about my life are to be listened to and acknowledged. These insights are also part of the fabric of how I can get well and become whole physically, emotionally, and spiritually."*

What was brought to the individuals in this study that we can bring to our relationships? Why did the interactions between the Behavioral Engagement facilitators and these study participants have successful outcomes? It was the application of new, proven ways of communicating and relating to another person that can create deeply satisfying relationships.

The Tenets and Philosophy of Behavioral Engagement

The model of Behavioral Engagement as a philosophy is grounded in science, and when applied correctly is an art. There are basic tenets about the nature of relationships and communication that are essential to the application of the model, which approaches both relationships and communication from a whole-person perspective.

➤ We enter into the application of BE without agendas, expectations, desired outcomes, or the idea of changing another person.

➤ We all want to be seen, heard, and valued for who we are. We want to be in relationships with those who validate our worth.

➤ Respect, acceptance, integrity of thought and action, and holding others in a sacred way are powerfully healing and transforming behaviors.

➤ Individuals often choose to make behavioral changes after their beliefs, values, and behavioral decisions are respected, acknowledged, and accepted.

➤ No one welcomes being told what they should do or what is best for them to do. They will likely resist. Once the interaction is not focused on the client's self-determination, the individual is likely to emotionally disconnect.

➤ The Golden Rule is the *physics* of relationships.[18]

➤ When our behaviors are congruent with our values, we have positive self-esteem. When our behaviors are not congruent with our values, our self-esteem is diminished and our behaviors express that.

➤ People will most often do what they want to do and will not do what they do not want to do, even when others think they should.

➤ An individual must experience an emotional shift before making a behavioral change for that change to be sustainable. People will generally make behavioral changes only if they believe that the level of pain or threat they are experiencing—which is the impetus for them to make a behavioral change—*is severe enough to warrant the level of discomfort they anticipate they will experience in making that behavior change.*

➤ Unless the *reactive mind,* which provokes our stored internal pain and fear response, is re-informed, random external stimuli can reactivate stored fear or pain responses and their accompanying adaptive behaviors.

➤ Not all *bad* behavior is bad. We often develop behaviors that are not optimal to avoid behaviors that are more harmful. Everyone is doing the best they can, even if their best is not too good.

➤ Behaviors are not changed with cognitive thinking. *Habits* can be changed with thought, intention, and process. However, emotional triggers can restimulate an individual's dormant behavior until they *emotionally choose* to release the behavior because it no longer serves their survival, whether physically, nutritionally, environmentally, or spiritually.

➤ No one heals or fixes anyone. Only we heal ourselves. Others can only *facilitate* this healing.

➤ It is a privilege to be in a relationship with another person. Relationships are sacred—worthy of reverence and respect.

Behavioral Engagement brings to relationship communications what we refer to as *Pure Presence—a state of being fully and wholly present*. It integrates the twenty relational dynamics detailed in the upcoming chapter that result in BE-ing and communicating with another person from our *whole self*, attentive and focused on the person in front of us, without bringing an agenda, anticipated responses, or desired outcomes to the interaction. *Pure presence* brings compassionate, respectful, and sacred interaction, which establishes the worth of what *both participants* bring to the relationship, rather than placing one of the individuals in a greater or lesser role than the other.

The dynamics of Behavioral Engagement have been studied and proven to be essential for successful behavioral change in both health-care-related interactions and in personal, familial, or work-based relationships. Autonomy, equality, sacredness, intention, and service to others all play important roles in creating the *Pure Presence* component of Behavioral Engagement.

Testing the Details

In researching Behavioral Engagement, hospitals and medical environments are used as testing sites. What is also used to assist in the ongoing development and testing of the model are NIWH students, who are required to participate in case study externships to demonstrate their ability to apply the model in their work with clients. The student externships provide an excellent opportunity to test specific aspects of Behavioral Engagement and to evaluate how each aspect impacts the student's professional and personal relationships.

Testing the specific aspects of BE requires two groups of externs that are provided different skill sets, which they are asked to use with their clients. One group is provided training in mindful listening, rapport building, interviewing skills, and goal-setting techniques. Another group of externs are provided the same set of skills the first group of externs is trained in. However, in addition to the first set of skills, the second group is trained in the Behavioral Engagement *Pure Presence* skills and components. The second group then applies both sets of skills to their interaction with their clients.

We surveyed both sets of externship students using the standardized Royal College of General Practitioners, Scotland, CARE Measure survey, adapted for the purposes of measuring Behavioral Engagement.[19]

The outcomes for the first group of non–Behavioral Engagement–trained externs scored, on average, positive for seven out of ten questions. The group of externs using the BE skills scored, on average, positive for nine out of the ten questions.

The difference in the two skill sets changed what the externs brought to the exchange with their clients. Depending upon the skill set they were trained in, there were significant differences in the extern's intention, attitude, expectations, state of presence, and the specific communication skills they brought to the client encounters. Then the group of externs that had *not* been trained in the BE skill set were given instructions in the model of *Pure Presence* and asked to apply these new skills, along with the first set of skills, to three additional clients.

When the CARE Measure surveys for the re-trained externs were completed, the scores were consistent and surprising. Expecting the scores to be equal to those of the first group trained in the full BE model, which had positively scored nine out of ten consistently, the group of externs who had been *re-trained* in the BE model scored a positive ten out of ten questions on the surveys.

We asked the twice-trained externs what shifted for them after the second training. They replied that the experience provided them with an organic understanding of how the specific nuances of the two different skill sets affected their communication *and* their relationship with the clients. They preferred the full *Pure Presence* skill set, as they personally experienced its transformational ability and now also *understood the science* behind why and how it worked so well. They also reported that it was more fulfilling for them, and their clients, to provide the *Pure Presence* skills to their interactions rather than applying just the listening skills, interviewing techniques, rapport, and goal-setting methods.

Let's Get Started

In the upcoming chapter we explore and learn how to apply the Behavioral Engagement model, with its *Pure Presence* components. Readers, who want information on the most current statistics relating to problematic behaviors in the United States, or the effect of culture and environment on our behaviors, are invited to read Part II of the book before beginning this next chapter.

We now have a basic understanding of the how and why of behaviors. In the next chapter we go directly to applying Behavioral Engagement and transforming our relationships.

(1) What has been valuable about reading where human behavior comes from? How has the connection between our emotions and survival instincts been helpful to you?

(2) How has this information assisted you in appreciating or better understanding any of your own behaviors or the behaviors of others you know?

(3) In what way does understanding how we develop our behaviors as forms of self-preservation and protection allow you to have a greater sense of compassion for some of the behaviors of others?

(4) How has this information helped you understand your own behaviors and how they have developed in your life?

(5) What information or insights has led you to rethink your opinion of someone you may be at odds with?

(6) Did any of this information cause you to reflect on how *we are all doing our best,* given our conditioning or upbringing?

(7) In what way do you think this information may shift your awareness of your own behaviors?

Chapter Two
Behavioral Engagement and *Pure Presence*

"I've learned that people will forget what you said, people will forget what you did, but people will not forget how you make them feel."
—Maya Angelou

What do you remember about your childhood, your first love, early school experiences, work experience, or your best friend? If you close your eyes and recall some of those memories, you will find it is the *feelings* you remember, and the pleasant feelings are the ones you want to revisit, not the painful ones.

Addressing behavioral change is no different. As human beings, we find all change stressful. It requires adaptation and learning new strategies for a new job, relationship, living environment, or activity. We want to avoid the stress of change and remain in *the known* where we have identified and defined our adaptation strategies to suit our comfort level.

As we now know, we think and act from our feelings, our beliefs, our values, and our worldview. W. H. Auden's words, *"We would rather be ruined than changed"* are a powerful statement about how deeply we are connected to our coping and behavioral mechanisms. Knowing this allows us to accept that we must identify and use new tools to create more fulfilling relationships.

Albert Einstein's well-known quote, *"You cannot solve a problem with the same level of thinking that created it,"* also applies. For most of us, if we want to transform our relationships, we must be willing to enter into them in a different way. We might consider starting with new information and, in addition, a new set of skills to solve the problems we are experiencing within our relationships.

Short-term change requires only short-term motivation to be present. For long-term or sustainable change to take place, the BE research demonstrates an important *process* that must take place. Namely, we must have the experience of having *what we think* integrate with *what we feel*. This integration can provide us with a new perspective and *emotional shifting* that can lead to self-directed and sustainable behavioral changes for both our relationships and health behaviors.

A good example of this is financial planning. In 2002, the Consumer Federation of America reported its findings that before the September 11, 2001, terrorist attack on the World Trade Center, many Americans did not consider financial planning as important as they did just one year after the terrorist attack.

What the event did was integrate what they had thought—*"Financial planning is not that important"*—with what their feelings were after the terrorist attack—*"It feels important to be better financially prepared for unforeseen events that can affect my sense of security."*[1]

Using or applying BE requires a willingness to let go of many conscious and unconscious self-focused concerns, thoughts, and behaviors. There is also a need, as the first step to changing our behavior in relationships, to become familiar with the transformative components found in the Behavioral Engagement model. These components allow for, and invite, the emotional shifting experience that is necessary for greater self-efficacy, self-awareness, and lasting behavioral change to occur.

The Components of *Pure Presence*

At the core of Behavioral Engagement is *Pure Presence*—a state of being fully and wholly present to another person. The components of *Pure Presence* are multidimensional and *whole-person* focused. They include multiple aspects that, when applied as an integrated approach to interpersonal communication, facilitate lasting behavioral change in ourselves and in others. The following aspects will be discussed individually, in detail, throughout this chapter:

- Sacredness of Relationships—worthy of reverence and respect
- Intention—what we want from the encounter
- Overlapping Brain State—when emotion and thought connect
- Skilled Listening—beyond hearing words
- Centered Body Language—creating an environment for personal discernment without distraction
- Biochemistry of Eye Contact—the windows to the soul
- Respectful Inquiry—exploring but not probing
- Compassion—the Golden Rule
- Authentic Collaboration—avoiding manipulation
- Valuing Silence Between Words—allowing for the dots to connect
- Demystified Information—clarity of how and why
- Focused Attention—focus on other with non-distracted presence
- Heart-Centered Presence—open to experiencing our humanity
- The Four Questions—what we all seek answers to
- Acceptance—of self and others without judgment
- Equality—holding yourself as equal with others
- Egoless Presence—letting go of control
- No-Trace Camping—leaving no traces of self
- Emotional Shifting—the "aha" moment
- Self-Awareness—self-assessment and insight

The Sacredness of Relationships

The word *sacredness* means "worthy of respect; venerable." We can easily find sacredness in all forms of nature, in our families, in what is dear to us, and in those we love. It can be a bit more challenging to see or feel the sacredness of everyday interactions with those who do not share our values, beliefs, or worldview. It is challenging, but when we become able to experience that each interaction with another person is an opportunity to learn and grow—and that it is a privilege to be in relationship with another person—then we and the other individual both experience the meaning and fulfillment of a sacred relationship.

In our overscheduled, frenetic society our awareness and experience of the sacredness of life, and of relationships, is often lost. The absence of sacredness does not eliminate the desire and need to have this important value present in our relationships and in our daily lives.

In Relationships It Boils Down to Our Intentions

In transforming relationships with BE the most important factor determining the success of this unique skills set is *intention.* Often we are not aware of our hidden or unconscious agendas, or that we are judging or blaming the person we are in relationship with. Being willing to take a step back from a desired outcome—such as having someone else change the way they are behaving—we can gain perspective on what is motivating us, or what our intentions are in the way we interact with others.

It cannot be overstated that *autonomy* is what each of us desire. We wish to be self-governed, not manipulated. When our intent for using Behavioral Engagement, or any other skill set, is to strengthen or transform our relationship, it should start with the understanding that we first need to look at our own behavior within that relationship. This starts by making changes to *how we behave* rather than trying to change the way someone else is behaving. If our intent is focused on convincing someone they should change their behavior despite their steadfast refusal to do so, we should expect to fail in our efforts.

Focusing on Brain Waves

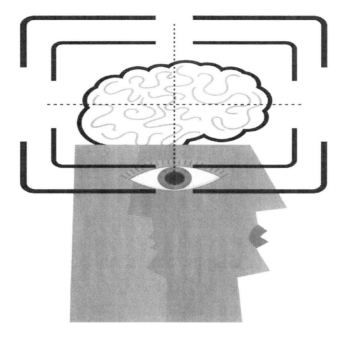

Step One in learning Behavioral Engagement skills is to understand the brain science upon which the model is based. Chapter 1 provided a simple overview of brain function and how each area has its own tasks to perform. In addition, each part of the brain produces *brain waves* that vary and are related to distinct functions as well.[2]

Our thinking, problem-solving, and *doing* brain is the cortical *beta wave* brain. This multi-tasking specialist has a rapid brain-wave speed that produces alertness, quick responses, and the ability to focus. Some medications for attention deficit disorder target—and increase—beta-wave activity to enhance the person's ability to focus. Conversely, if our beta waves are too ramped up, we can experience insomnia, elevated blood pressure, or anxiety.

The *alpha* brain waves are considerably slower than the beta waves, and generally come from the mid-portion of our brain. Alpha waves allow the mind to be clear and internally focused, with the body relaxed and calm. Most of us are familiar with that wonderfully relaxed, twilight state just before we fall asleep or when we wake up in the night with a great idea or thoughts that seem to be pouring out of us.

If we do not write the thoughts or ideas down, we realize in the morning that they are *gone,* and we cannot retrieve them even though last night we experienced brilliant clarity and awareness that now eludes us. That clarity comes from the intersection of the two levels of brain functioning.

The slower alpha waves appear to be a gateway for imparting and accessing information in our midbrain or limbic region. This area is generally referred to as our *subconscious* brain. Children spend much of their time in an alpha or theta brain-wave state. Since the theta-wave state allows the brain to absorb and retain large amounts of information and stimuli, children can easily learn new information.

The theta brain waves are even slower than the alpha waves and are a normal brain-wave state for children or sleeping adults. Although theta brain waves are found in adult brains, their frequency decreases with aging as there is less need to gather and store information.

Adults can experience the theta state during deep meditation. We know children are more spontaneous and *tuned in* than older adults. It is through these brain-wave functions that sensory motor information imprints the brain's *hard drive* and produces the adaptation responses discussed in the previous chapter.

The environmental impact on a child's emotional development is strongest between the ages of birth and pre-puberty, beginning around age eight or nine years old. After the age of nine, most children begin to develop rudimentary androgens, or sex hormones, that mature in full-blown puberty. It is this biochemical change that begins transforming the child's theta-wave brain function toward an adult state of beta-wave brain function.

In this transition, the child's slower brain-wave states recede and the faster beta-wave states increase. Thus the data-gathering, *theta-wave child brain transforms* from a subconscious dominant brain wave to the conscious, thinking, *rapid beta-wave adult brain state*. This beta-wave brain state allows for greater intellectual work compared with the earlier theta states, when the child's brain is taking in vast amounts of information and neurological stimuli from its environment.

Overlapping Brain State

Of course, there is much overlap between the conscious and unconscious *minds,* if you will. Many of us have experienced driving somewhere while thinking about an event we are planning, working through an idea, or pondering a relationship situation. Suddenly and unexpectedly we find ourselves at our destination, unable to remember passing the post office where we made a right turn or the coffee shop on the corner.

This is an example of conscious and unconscious mind overlap, and it occurs all the time. The busier or more distracted we are by our fast-paced beta brain, the less we are aware of that overlap. BE invites the integration of this conscious and unconscious state by the way we are present to the other person.

Pure Presence, which is the foundation of Behavioral Engagement, facilitates the individual's accessing and integrating their stored wisdom, information, and memory. This integration provides the "aha" moments of new awareness. This new awareness is the result of the union of the conscious beta brain information and the subconscious alpha-theta brain information.

Slowing the beta brain down and promoting an environment for it to overlap with the alpha brain invites new insights, awareness, and self-efficacy. The skills of BE allow this expansive experience to take place. This is accomplished by the facilitator being fully present to the other person physically and emotionally—in a centered, relaxed, receptive, attentive, respectful, and compassionate way.

Skilled Listening

"Are you listening?" When was the last time you asked that question? When was the last time someone really listened to you? Were they fully present, making soft eye contact, being calm and still, paying attention to you and focusing on what you had to say? Or were they distracted or preoccupied?

Did you see their eyes glaze over for a moment or two when they moved their focus from you to some internal dialogue they were having? Many of us have had the experience during conversations of realizing the other person is sitting there thinking about something other than what we are sharing with them.

That person may be thinking about what she or he is going to say next, or developing a response to what we are talking about before we have even finished speaking. This can result in our not feeling heard or not cared about, and can potentially re-stimulate the memory of a similar hurtful experience. Often, it is this type of re-stimulation that can derail our communications and relationships.

The opposite of this type of "listening" is *skilled listening*, which is intentional listening that incorporates the twenty dimensional skills and tools that make up the *Pure Presence* of Behavioral Engagement. When we incorporate these skills, we learn how we can listen deeply and comprehend on intellectual, emotional, and spiritual levels what the individual is communicating and sharing with us. Skilled listening is hearing the *whole person*—and understanding what they are communicating *with our whole self.*

Mind Wandering

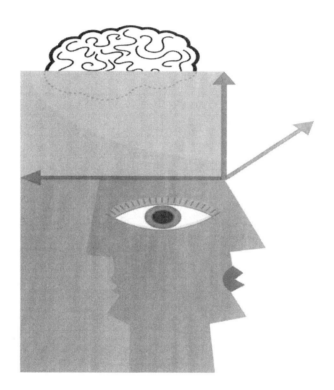

A study by Harvard researchers Gilbert and Killingsworth, published in the November 10, 2010, journal *Science,* reveals that 46.9% of people are "mind wandering."[3] This means that almost half the time we spend communicating with each other, we, or the other person, are not listening to what is being said. When we go to the movies we sit, watch, and listen, paying close attention to details, dialogue, body language, and behavior. We are more tuned in when we watch a movie than much of the time when we relate to the significant people in our lives. *Pure presence* for the Behavioral Engagement facilitator is like being present to, and watching, an engaging movie. Your attention is totally focused on the person in front of you and the story he or she is sharing with you.

Unfortunately, our society is now becoming increasingly narcissistic. It is so prevalent and commonplace that narcissism has been declassified and removed in 2013 from the American Psychological Association's *Diagnostic and Statistical Manual of Mental Disorders* as a personality disorder.[4]

These days, having someone's *Pure Presence* is rare. We know our therapist will anticipate the clock hour, our doctor has limited time to spend, and other health professionals have similar concerns that impose on our communications with them. Where BE is applied in health care settings, even with office visit time constraints, the skills of being *purely present* to another person can transform the quality of health care delivery and reconnect us with the art of relationship.

Centered Body Language

We start the process of providing pure, unconditional presence with centering our body in a comfortable posture. Our focus and intent is on listening to the other person, with no distractions. We listen to the other person without interjecting our thoughts between the person's words, or forming judgments about what she or he is saying. At the same time we are being *purely present* to this person, we are also appreciating the privilege of hearing their story, of their sharing thoughts and feelings with us. We are in a state of being fully engaged and wholly present to this person.

We begin each Behavioral Engagement exchange with a comfortable, relaxed, and neutral body posture. This is referred to as *centered body language*, because we are sitting with our body centered in the chair, our feet uncrossed on the floor, and our hands relaxed on the arms of the chair. Your legs, ankles, and arms are never crossed, as this communicates an emotionally *closing off* gesture to the other person.

If the chair you are sitting in does not allow you to have your forearms resting on the arms in a relaxed manner, you can hold an object, such as a cup or glass, in your hands, but at no point should you allow the object to distract you. Why? We enter into BE with the intention of creating a physical presence for the other person that does not, in any way, visually or verbally disrupt them from potentially experiencing self-discernment.

If you are distracted, or if you are distracting the person by drinking, scratching, moving around, or playing with your hair or eyeglasses, what you are communicating with your body language, and lack of presence, is that you are not actually listening to them—that you have other things on your mind besides being present to this individual.

When training health professionals, we videotape their interactions with clients so they can see what their posture, eye contact, and body language are communicating. It is very helpful to objectively see yourself on videotape to understand just why the specifics of this behavioral change model are so important. If you have a friend who would like to learn Behavioral Engagement along with you, you can videotape your interactions and use the tape as a tutorial to assist both of you in perfecting your BE skills. When we step away from a conversation and observe the body signals passing between two individuals, we can see immediately if they are listening, or being listened to. You can also easily understand the nonverbal communication that is transpiring between them.

When your posture is centered and you are not leaning forward or back, and are emotionally relaxed and focused, this indicates to the other person that you are fully present and *in the moment* with him or her. Leaning forward can make the person feel that you are being aggressive, overtly assertive, or perhaps trying to take control of the exchange. If you are leaning away, it may feel like you are communicating judgment, criticism, or rejection.

Your calm, relaxed stillness provides an environment that is both nonthreatening and conveys a lack of expectation or desire to control the interaction. Although you will be responsive—smiling, nodding, and thanking the client as he or she shares the information—you will not be probing, asking questions, exploring motives, making comments, or giving opinions. In personal relationships we all want to express our feelings without being interrupted or *edited* by the people with whom we are communicating.

This requires us to not think in any way about our own concerns. It also requires us to not be distracted physically, emotionally, or environmentally. This is letting go of our own story to listen to and be present to another person's communication. This can be very difficult to do when we have *wants* or *seek attention* within the relationship. You may want this person to agree with you, care about you, take your advice, or fulfill emotional or practical needs.

If our own need fulfillment is the objective when we enter a conversation, or if we have an agenda and want someone else to change for our purposes, the likelihood is that the other individual, on some level, *feels* this intent. When someone gets that we are focused on our own need fulfillment, they withdraw as a natural reaction to not wanting us to expect, ask, or demand that they change to accommodate our needs. Despite solid evidence of why it would be a good idea to make changes in our behaviors, we do not want to do it unless it comes from our own decision-making process. The change must also be what we believe will make our lives better, safer, or more meaningful.

The way we look at someone, the way we sit or communicate through our body language, reveals far more about our thoughts and intentions than most of us realize. Several years ago I was working at a Boston-area hospital, training nurses in the Behavioral Engagement model, and we were filming the interactions between the mock clients and the nurses before they received the BE training.

When the videos were played back and the nurses saw how they communicated with their clients, they were shocked. We then provided a demonstration of both an effective and a noneffective way of being present and explained the science of what the nurses were revealing through their eye contact, the way they spoke to the client, and what their body movements were telegraphing.

The nurses then personally experienced a one-to-one interview session with another nurse using the Behavioral Engagement and *Pure Presence* model. The newly trained nurses took the BE experience back to their patients, coworkers, and families, and reported significant improvement in their communications, not only with patients, but also with their children, their colleagues, their spouses, and other significant relationships where they applied the BE skills.

Windows to the Soul

We have heard the expression *"The eyes are the windows to the soul."* If the unconscious is accepted to be the human soul, then indeed this is an accurate statement, as the eyes do reflect our unconscious mind. When we look into someone's eyes, we are looking at communications from the limbic-amygdala portion of their brain.

Through subtle pupil, eye muscle, and facial muscle responses, the feelings recorded in our midbrain are revealed. The brain stem and cranial nerves communications are responsible for this transparency.[5] In spite of our attempts to hide that we are lying, upset, or even in love, our nervous system once again reveals the inner truth through subtle neurological body language.

During your entire exchange with the other person, you hold soft eye contact or look at their eyes, even if they are looking away or not looking directly at you. Why? Soft eye contact is one of the most essential components of *Pure Presence*. The neurology of eye contact is a remarkable conduit for the intersection of our feeling-sensory-motor brain and our cortical-thinking brain.

The Eyes Have It

The eye and its optic nerve are an extension of the brain stem that runs parallel along both sides of the limbic portion of the brain. The limbic region of the brain is considered to be *the center of emotions in human beings.* In many love songs, eye contact is described to communicate the expression of emotions more powerful than words.

The eyes are so intimately connected with our sensory motor survival system that if we look into someone's eyes and see danger, our *fight or flight* hormones are immediately secreted because of the perceived fear. The opposite is true when we look into someone's eyes and see kindness, caring, or love. Then our brain produces oxytocin, a hormone that responds to feelings of trust and love.[6]

By holding soft, accepting eye contact with another person, you provide a safe and caring environment. This invites the other person to let go of their fear of possibly being judged, evaluated, or expected to meet some standard that she or he is unaware of. By being relaxed and centered, you reinforce the other person's experience of feeling comfortable, safe, and valued.

If the person does not keep eye contact with you at first, remain relaxed while continuing to hold soft eye contact with that person's eyes. They will feel and respond to your attention, and will shortly begin to make sustained eye contact with you. If you look away and then back at the person, it is a signal that your thoughts and mind are wandering.

If you have ever been at a cocktail party speaking with an acquaintance who is constantly looking to see who is arriving, you know exactly how this makes someone feel. If we are truly listening to someone, our eyes are focused on them, not elsewhere.

When a person is learning to horseback ride, they are instructed to pay close attention to where they are looking, since a horse will move in the same direction the rider is looking. This is because of the subtle and amazing communication signals being sent from the rider's hands and body directly to the horse's body. How and where you look during your communications tells the other person a great deal about your intentions and where your thoughts are.

Respectful Inquiry

When we respectfully inquire about or reflect what another person has said, it helps both parties reinforce a clear understanding of what each person is trying to communicate. Reflective inquiry also communicates the level of attention we are giving to the exchange, or the shared thoughts and feelings.

This simple skill helps strengthen the relationship through clearer communication and understanding. It also helps create greater intimacy. By restating what we understood the other person has shared with us, and by asking for confirmation that our understanding of what they said is what they intended to communicate, we keep the exchange transparent and clarified.

Here is an example:

You are speaking with your sister, with whom you currently have a conflict. You want to bring up a subject that is important for both of you to discuss in order to resolve that conflict, but you are aware that this is a potentially volatile topic of discussion. When you speak about the subject, rather than talking about how upset you were by what happened, you can approach it by asking how she feels, and then sharing your desire to resolve the conflict and get your relationship back on track.

It is important to think about how it would feel if you were sitting opposite your sister and she was dialoguing with you about the incident. What might she say or how might she say it that would create a desire in you to reconcile with her rather than continue feeling the hurt or resentment? What would the tone of her voice sound like? What type of words would be inviting rather than provocative? By approaching the discussion with a sense of inquiry, rather than with an intention to air grievances, conflicts can be more easily resolved.

The Golden Rule

The Golden Rule is a wonderful guide for how to behave toward others.
In the NIWH health-professional training program, the philosophy courses present the Golden Rule as it is found in various world cultures and religions.

The teachings of most traditional religions and philosophies are grounded in wisdom handed down through a prophetic being whose teachings essentially documented the cause-and-effect outcomes of specific behaviors. For instance, if we behave in a particular way, then a likely outcome, or response from others, will generally occur. The intent of this wisdom is to teach followers how to live a good life. These observations evolved into belief systems.

As found in the Bible's 2 Corinthians 4:16, most ancient religions observed the same "common good" cause-and-effect phenomenon: "He which soweth sparingly shall reap sparingly; He which soweth bountifully shall reap bountifully."

This same phenomenon is shared with the well-known Golden Rule and is observed in the following beliefs and faiths:

Judaism—What is hateful to you, do not to your fellowman. That is the entire law; all the rest is commentary.

Talmud, Shabbat 31a

Islam—No one of you is a believer until he desires for his brother that which he desires for himself.

Sunnah

Confucianism—Surely it is the maxim of loving kindness: Do not unto others what you would not have them do unto you.

Analects 15:23

Brahmanism—This is the sum of duty: Do naught unto others which would cause you pain if done to you.

Mahabharata 5:1517

Buddhism—Hurt not others in ways that you yourself would find hurtful.

Udana-Varga 5:18

Christianity—All things whatsoever ye would that men should do to you, do ye even so to them; for this is the law and the prophets.

Matthew 7:12

Taoism—Regard your neighbor's gain as your own gain and your neighbor's loss as your own loss.

T'ai Shang Kan Ying P'ien

Zoroastrianism—That nature alone is good which refrains from doing unto another whatsoever is not good for itself.

Dadistan-i-dinik 94:5

Authentic Collaboration

Raymond George Hunt, an applied psychologist and former professor emeritus at the State University of New York, Buffalo, has said that there is *"quite a thin line that separates collaboration from manipulation."*[7]

This statement is especially helpful when it comes to our interactions within relationships. Often we think we are behaving collaboratively, acting respectfully, or that we do not have an agenda going into an interaction when, indeed, we are working toward an outcome that serves our needs or desires.

It is made clear, and repeated often, to the health care professionals we train that being aware of our intentions is the single most important responsibility we each have toward another person. Living in today's world we are bombarded by various attempts to influence our behaviors, so much so that this now blatant manipulation is taken for granted.

It has become all too easy for us to try to influence the choices of others, especially within our personal relationships, where our needs and desires are strong. It is important, as we saw in the previous chapter, to self-assess and be aware of what our motives and intentions are as we enter into discussions and dialogues with *each* of our relationships.

Silence Between Words

In addition to being centered, relaxed, focused, fully present, respectful, and compassionate, one of the most important aspects of Behavioral Engagement is valuing the spaces, or silence, between verbal exchanges. When we allow the space between the spoken words to be uninterrupted, the overlap and integration of the beta and alpha brain—the conscious and unconscious *minds*—have an opportunity to connect and integrate.

It is in this special space of silence, or stillness, that we can change our understanding in both our feeling and our thinking brain. This new, multi-level awareness can lead to discerning organic, self-directed behavioral change. In applying Behavioral Engagement, it is best to allow *four* full seconds to transpire between verbal exchanges. At first you will have to count to four in your mind.

Very shortly, you will have an intuitive sense of the *time in the silence*. You will know when the other person is ready to move on, as they may look away to signal that they have finished sharing their thoughts or feelings with you. More important, *they may begin to speak again* to express thoughts or feelings they are now synthesizing as a result of an "overlapping brain" experience.

You continue to hold soft eye contact, possibly nodding, smiling, or responding with facial expressions, but *not speaking*. To interrupt this stillness, to interject ourselves into this space, robs the other person of the opportunity to connect their own dots, to understand themselves more deeply, and to be able to integrate the feeling and thinking information necessary to make the emotional shift that is critical to sustaining lasting change in their life or their relationships.

No one heals, cures, fixes, re-directs, or changes another person. All change comes from internal emotional shifting that must originate from a personal discernment process the individual experiences, or it has no lasting value. To acknowledge and respect this process, and allow it to provide authentic self-awareness is one of the steps in facilitating Behavioral Engagement.

Attempting to tell someone why they should change and emphasizing what the consequences are of not changing does not work. It does not work in medicine, which is why the issue of compliance—of patients following their doctor's "orders"—is the number-one problem in the practice of medicine today. Trying to tell someone what to do does not work in personal relationships, either.

We want to be invited to discern and figure out for ourselves what the best course of action is *for us* to take in a given situation. Unless we are in an acute, life-threatening situation, we do not want other people making those decisions for us. We want shared decision making with our health care professionals, as well as with our intimate relationships. We want what we know about ourselves and our needs to be respected. We want what we feel to matter.

Demystified Information

One important tool for facilitating a patient's health behavior change is the use of demystified health information. Just a few years ago, a report from the Institutes of Medicine said that more than 90 million Americans are health illiterate and do not understand the most basic health information needed to prevent illness.[8]
Just as patients *"cannot change old behavior without new information,"* within our relationships we need new information to respond or behave differently.

This new information comes from two main sources. The first source is from clear and respectful communication of our feelings. Because others cannot read our mind or know our feelings, it is essential in creating successful relationships that we are willing to express and share our feelings without provoking conflict. This is best achieved through using "I" statements. "I" statements or "I" messages are an approach to communicating with another person about a problem that does not suggest or imply, in any way, that they are the cause of the problem. "I" statements are a nonjudgmental alternative to "you" statements, which often suggest or imply possible blame or judgment of the other person, and can cause negative emotional triggering.

The second form of new information comes from the *brain overlap* experience. With this experience, we are able to connect our beta and alpha brain-wave function and arrive at a new integrated awareness, potential clarity, or motivation that can lead to authentic, sustainable behavioral changes.

Focused Attention

When we are experiencing *focused attention*, we are fully engaged with who or what is in front of us. We are not distracted physically or emotionally. We are not moving around, shaking our legs or arms, playing with our hair or eyeglasses, scratching, eating, or drinking, but instead are calm, relaxed, focused on the other person, and communicating a centered body language. It is important not to be distracting. Being physically distracting or preoccupied, paying attention to ourselves rather than paying attention to the person we are with, can communicate a lack of attention or interest in the other person. It can also be viewed or experienced as a self-absorbed or narcissistic behavior.

Heart Centered, Not Head Centered

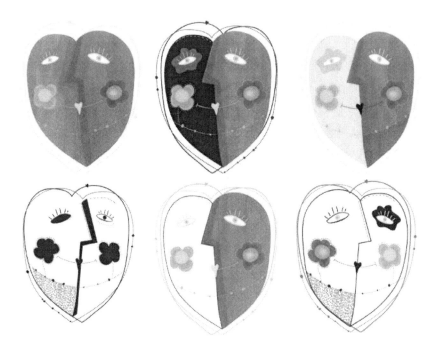

The program we developed for hospital nurses is titled *Creating a Renaissance of Relationship-Centered Care.*[9] For our health professionals, doing the work of BE and *Pure Presence* is a calling and a vocation; it goes beyond just having a career or a way to earn a living. In the words of Sir Winston Churchill, *"We make a living by what we get—we make a life by what we give."*

Although Behavioral Engagement may not be part of your work, it can be an important part of your life. It will change and transform not only your relationships, but also how you live in the world and what you give to others. This is work *from the heart* that desires to give and receive the highest good for both the other individual and yourself within the relationship.

Our research findings confirm that Behavioral Engagement is as potent in shifting family dynamics and personal and professional relationships as it is in transforming the health behaviors of the hospital study patients.

The Four Questions

A brilliant study out of the University of Washington, School of Medicine identified the four most important questions patients want answered by their health care providers.[10] These questions give us insight into what the important questions are in our personal relationships as well.

The first question the researchers identified was *"Are you listening to me?"* How many times have you gone to a medical or dental appointment and really wondered if in between the intercom buzzing, the practitioner stepping out of their office, and cell phone interruptions, he or she is not really listening to what you are saying? This type of experience can produce anxiety, frustration, and the feeling that we are not valued or respected.

The best example of not being heard is when we are having a conversation with someone, their cell phone rings, and they answer it—or they start texting while we are trying to communicate with them.

Being interrupted in a conversation, or being with someone who is distracted while we are interacting with them, causes *us* to be less emotionally present and less engaged *with them.*

The second question is specific to health care providers, but can easily be interpreted for personal conversations. *"How did this happened to me?"* The answers we are looking for in our health care relationships are different from those in our personal relationships, but the question remains the same.

This question relates to the individual trying to understand the specifics of what *they did* to find themselves in this particular situation. Often with our health issues the answer lies with our lifestyle choices. The Harvard School of Public Health and other research studies have shown that 70% of all chronic diseases are preventable through lifestyle-behavior change. This includes adult diabetes, heart disease, and cancer. In personal relationships, we also want to understand, *"How did this happen to me? What did I do to have this outcome occur?"*

In addition to understanding the how and why of a situation, each of us wants to be in control of our lives. Although there is not much information to explain why random things happen, or why our life takes the course it does, we are strongly invested in *understanding and controlling as much as we can about our lives*. In our personal relationships, the question we are asking each other is *"Why did this happen to me?"* In other words, *"Did how I behaved make him or her stop loving me, or get me fired … or even make me sick?"*

What we also know from our personal experiences is that our friends *really* do not want our advice. If a friend complains about his fiancée and plans to call the wedding off—and we are foolish enough to agree that his fiancée is not a paragon of virtue—we *know* as soon as they make up that we are in "hot water" with our friend. He will tell the fiancée what we said, then not talk to us because he is mad that we said something unpleasant about his beloved. No one *really* wants advice, or to be told, or hear suggestions about how to behave—not even from our doctors. We want to be *listened to* so we can try to figure things out ourselves.

Most often with our health, what we want is for the pain to go away or the fear that something is seriously wrong with us to be negated, but we really don't want *advice*. We want the opportunity to talk things through. And unless we are in a lot of pain, or have a lot of fear about the symptoms we are experiencing, what we are looking for is the *information* or the specific tests that can tell us what might be causing our problem.

In our relationships, this is helpful information. *No one wants us to tell them what we think they should or should not do, or how they should or should not feel.* They want us to listen, with compassion, without judgment, and without opinions. They want us to be there for them but not interject ourselves into their process of figuring things out for themselves.

Behavioral Engagement provides individuals with what they are seeking in relationships—safety, comfort, respect, compassion, and equality—without interjecting ourselves into their story. The BE protocol has been successfully used in clinical environments to serve individuals receiving health care services. It has also demonstrated its ability to assist in transforming the dynamics of personal, professional, and intimate relationships.

The third question applies across all relational boundaries. *"Do you care what I know about my condition, or situation, or are you just going to tell me what you think you know about it?"* When we seek counsel of any kind, from a friend or even a physician, we want *our* experience and knowledge about the situation or condition to be valued, respected, and considered.

Anything less suggests that what we know, as the expert of ourselves, is unimportant—when *what we know about ourselves* is most important. We want our wisdom and self-awareness to be acknowledged and valued, rather than having someone else presume to know what is happening to us.

The fourth question is also an important one: *"How I can control my situation?"* The question is not, *"Can you tell me what to do"* or *"Can you fix this,"* but *"How can I take control of my condition or situation?"* A person may not seek to be *cured* or *fixed* by their doctor any more than that person wants to be *advised* in his or her personal relationships. They want to be *listened to,* have their thoughts and feelings *valued,* and most important, they want the pain— along with the fear of what might be wrong with them—to go away.

It can be tempting to *advise* others, to share our own experience about a similar situation. When we do this, however, we are leaving our debris at the campsite, forgetting to *leave no trace* of our being there. When we provide this same respectfulness in relationships, and avoid interjecting ourselves into the other person's story or process, we are giving them *the gift of our Pure Presence.*

Equality

Human beings have an innate desire to experience fairness and justice. When we are treated with equality—*the state of being equal in status or value*—we also have the experience of being respected and valued, which we know is an essential need for all of us.

Many times we have the experience of being "one down" or "one up" with someone else. This juxtaposition creates competition and fearfulness. When we are not on equal footing, or of equal standing with another person, we feel less valued or respected.

Acceptance and Nonjudgment: A New Communication Tool

It is imperative to respect and accept the other individual's narrative or feelings by not interjecting ourselves into their dialogue with words like *I, me,* or *my.* Instead, we support the communication by using words such as *you* or *we* that stay focused on *their* perspective or story, unless it is important that we make a possessive "I feel" statement. Then, in order to share *our* feelings, which may refer to a previous conflict now being discussed, we might say something like *"What I was feeling then is …."*

With BE, is it always more effective *not* to interrupt the person we are interacting with, so they may completely explore and share their thoughts and feelings. Interruptions or interjections derail their self-discernment process and short-circuit the integration of their feelings with their thought process. Interrupting can also shut down or deflect what they wish to say or share with you.

Our research has shown that after someone has had the expansive experience of another person's *Pure Presence,* and of being deeply, respectfully accepted and listened to without interruption or distraction, that individual will innately reach out and listen to what the other person is feeling and experiencing. This is especially true with couples using Behavioral Engagement, as it can eliminate one of the major deterrents to intimate relationships. Yukio Ishizuka, MD, psychiatrist and author of *Breakthrough Intimacy: Sad to Happy through Closeness,* writes about this: *"Fear often arises when the couple reaches a new level of closeness and intimacy. When this increased closeness occurs, the partners can feel threatened or vulnerable because of a sense of [and fear of a] dependence they may feel towards the relationship."*[11]

BE skills create a safe, noncritical, nondependent environment within which the partners can feel comfortable discussing and understanding their reactions to a new level of intimacy.

It is important to remember, however, that BE is not *"talk therapy."* It is the *Pure Presence* of another person that allows us the experience of being wholly listened to, authentically heard, and accepted without judgment. It is akin to unconditional love that is given freely and without expectations, rather than conditional love that seeks to have us *perform* or fulfill another's needs in exchange for acceptance.

No-Trace Camping

During the training of our health professional students, one of the examples we use to illustrate *Pure Presence* and respect in our relationship communications is responsible camping. If you have never gone camping, the number-one rule is to leave the area you camped in the same way you found it. This is a sign of value and respect for nature and the beauty of the environment you have just enjoyed. This behavior is also recognition of the appropriateness of not leaving traces of ourselves all over the woods or in any natural environment we spend time in.

The sense of appropriate boundaries, and the avoidance of not interjecting ourselves into another's process, is not something that we tend to focus on in our current culture. However, just as with no-trace camping, practicing noninvasive communication means we do not leave our debris all over the person or the conversations we are having.

With no-trace camping we take away everything we have brought onto the site, and leave it just as we found it so that the next camper may enjoy the beauty, peace, and sacredness of the natural setting. In the same way, we want to practice *no-trace camping* within our relationships. Rather than allowing our ego needs to *leave their mark* on another person, Behavioral Engagement establishes, with its *Pure Presence,* the elimination of ego projection or personal agendas onto the other person. This respectful behavior elevates the relationship between the individuals and creates integrity, fostering authentic communication.

Self-Awareness and Self-Assessment

In Prochaska's Stages of Change, the self-assessment, self-evaluation tool is an important one. It is also found in a behavior-change model people are most familiar with. Alcoholics Anonymous was started in 1935 by two "hopeless alcoholics," Dr. Bob and Bill W. The program consists of twelve steps an individual takes to confront their problems and remedy their behaviors toward themselves and others.

The twelve-step process has been applied to dozens of other behaviors as well. Although the twelve-step model has received mixed reviews, the self-inventory tool, which produces self-awareness and a clarity of intention, has received much validation in the psychological community. Prochaska also points out that self-assessments are *"powerful tools for information and self-correction."* If the roots of change can be found in this basic step of self-awareness, why is it still so difficult for us to self-evaluate, recognize the need for change, and take the appropriate action steps?

Self-awareness is an important component of personal growth and change. However, without the experience of an emotional shifting necessary for us to change how we view the world, and what we believe is best for our quality of life or personal survival, self-awareness can be an intellectual process that does not lead to sustainable behavioral change.

Emotional Shifting

What is often called the *"aha"* moment is when an individual "gets" or organically understands the how and why of a situation or problem they have not been able to fully engage with or resolve. Teachers often speak about their students' *aha* moments when *the lightbulb goes off* in their heads and the students are able to take in knowledge or an awareness they did not previously comprehend. When we have these moments of awareness, we experience a shift in how we understand, or view, a previous experience of our self, another person, or the world around us. This emotional shifting informs what we believe about how to adapt or survive in our environment, or in relationship to others, and can have a profound effect on how we behave as a result.

Behavioral Engagement provides a unique way of being present to ourselves and then subsequently being present to others. It supports an authentic process of personal discernment, as well as the experience of important moments of realization and insight. These moments of discovery and new awareness need to occur on both a feeling and thinking level before we are able to shift our beliefs, emotions, and worldview—to make positive, sustainable behavioral change. Without this emotional shifting we are rooted to our adaptive emotional responses and vulnerable to those responses being triggered or re-stimulated.

Egoless Presence—the Behavioral Engagement Zone

Recently, one of the nurses taking the Behavioral Engagement training commented that she now realized that whatever emotional *leftovers* she brought from home to work in the hospital were immediately communicated to her patients, whether she wanted that to happen or not. Our eye contact and body language telegraph our feelings more than we realize. Therefore becoming aware of our *ego encroachments*, then counteracting them by staying centered and *"other"* focused rather than being self-focused, is a positive action we can take to continually improve our professional and personal relationships.

Another technique Behavioral Engagement practitioners use to *stay centered* is to rinse their hands and face with cool water before they meet with their next client. Then, they clear their mind of the last interaction they had by taking a moment or two to breathe deeply. This helps them to re-center themselves and re-focus before moving on to the next client. By being aware and mindful of the need to clear out unrelated thoughts and inner dialogue, these professionals have developed exceptional relationships with their clients and patients, and also transformed their personal relationships at home and at work using the same skills they were applying with their patients and clients. The same considerations apply when we are engaged in personal communication.

Filling our mind with thoughts and inner dialogue that trigger emotional responses does not allow us to be fully present to the other person. When we have these mental, emotional, or even physical distractions, we need to re-center ourselves, especially if we are having a dialogue with another person. Distractions significantly decrease the effectiveness and quality of our communication.

It is not easy to remain centered when we are engaged in personal dialogue that may have emotional charge or triggers for us. As we shared with the nurses and health professionals in their Behavioral Engagement training, it is critical that we *"leave our ego at the door"*[12] while bringing our whole, centered self to the interaction and communication with the other person.

Final Comments Before We Review the Steps of Behavioral Engagement

Before the mid-1980s our culture enjoyed a healthier, more simplistic lifestyle than it does today. In today's "grab and go" culture, which promises us greater convenience and luxury, we may have lost the more fulfilling aspects of life: the time to listen, to *BE* with ourselves and others, to connect with our humanity, and to enjoy the innate human need to be in relationship with others.

If we wish to transform our relationships, we need to remember that transformation begins with *our* behavior. Gandhi said, *"Be the change you wish to see in the world."* In the same way, we also need to become the change we wish to see in our relationships.

Many of us have lost our ability to take a step back from our intimate relationships and develop objectivity. The application of Behavioral Engagement will assist you in doing just that. Once you gain a fresh and objective look at your relationship interactions, you can create new behaviors with enthusiasm and commitment that will enhance the quality and fulfillment of all of your relationships.

It is time to review the steps for facilitating the Behavioral Engagement model and get ready to *graduate* from this new and exciting communication skills training. These twelve steps can help you immediately transform your relationships!

A Step-by-Step Review of Behavioral Engagement Skills

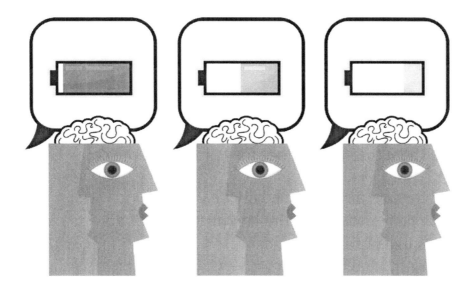

The purpose of Behavioral Engagement is to provide communication skills that will strengthen and enrich your relationships, and avoid having your interactions take a detour into conflict and misunderstanding. Whether you are interacting with your significant other, a coworker, your boss, your mother-in-law, or a friend, the skills of BE can be applied to all relationship communications.

STEP ONE: *Begin each communication by clearing away any distraction* we might be experiencing, and focus on the opportunity to have a shared exchange with another person or persons that will result in a positive outcome for both or for all the individuals participating. If you have had prior conflicts with any of the people you are interacting with, visualize placing conflicts aside, along with your own ego needs and see a positive, win-win outcome.

It is best to enter into this, or any communication, with the *intention* of a centered, receptive, respectful, mindful, nonjudgmental, fully present, compassionate state; be present to the other person as an equal, and *maintain this state of mutuality* throughout the communication.

STEP TWO: It is important to *be physically comfortable.* This will allow you to avoid becoming distracted and will facilitate relaxation. If you have a comfortable chair you like to sit in or are outside your home or office, it is helpful that what you are sitting on has a back to it so you may sit upright and centered. This allows for *a centered body posture during your communication*, and supports a centered, respectful and mindful presence to the other person or individuals.

This posture will relax you as well as the other person or persons, and assist you in remaining in *Pure Presence* throughout the communication. It is best to identify any physical distraction that might cause you to lose your attention, focus, or center. Before you begin your exchange you may want to **remove any distractions**, such as a ticking clock, or turn the ringer of the phone off.

Fidgeting, looking away, answering your cell phone, or focusing any physical attention on yourself will be distracting to the person you are with, and will communicate to them that you are not fully present in the conversation.

It is best not to schedule any other activity near or around the same time you wish to have your conversation, as the encroachment of outside distraction can derail your efforts to have a focused, centered conversation.

STEP THREE: After you are in your *centered body language* posture, your eye contact with the other person is the next step to facilitating *Pure Presence* in your communication. **Your sustained, eye contact is soft and soothing, without judgment and never aggressive or probing**. The way you look at the other person communicates your inner thoughts and dialogue. You want to be aware of this, as well as be centered in your thoughts and intentions. Your eye contact can create physiological responses in the other person that elevates trust, comfort, and the feeling of being accepted. These are ideal states to find ourselves in with our important relationships, especially those we wish to enhance and deepen.

STEP FOUR: *Check your intention*. Throughout your communication, keeping your intention open, centered, and nonjudgmental is an important part of creating the desired state of *Pure Presence* with the other person. If you begin to feel an emotional trigger, or an ego need surfacing, you can **mentally repeat the word intention** to help yourself become centered again.

Conversations with our intimate relationships can go off track because we lose our focus and then the opportunist "pop-ups"—just like on the computer—find their way into our thinking. Just as there are "pop-up" blockers on your computer, checking your intention will allow you to avoid being drawn away from your center and able to **remain purely present**. Distractions, both internal and external, can derail our communications. If your communication begins to go off track, you can immediately check if there is an agenda that may be unconsciously coming up for you. Example: You want an apology or you want to *"be right."*

STEP FIVE: If you requested or asked to have this conversation with the other person, you might begin the exchange with respectful inquiry, asking them their feelings about the matter that you wish to clarify. *For example*: *"Sweetheart, could you share or clarify the way you were feeling when we argued about going to your aunt's house for the holidays?"* **Once you ask your question, do NOT continue speaking**, but allow the other person the opportunity to gather their thoughts and respond to you. This also applies to workplace communications.

Your **intention and sustained, soft eye contact** will signal to them that you are sincerely interested in hearing how they feel and what they have to say. If you keep talking, or interrupt them, the conversation will become about *your* feelings and not theother person's. If you begin to feel anxious, re-center your intention and **check your centered body language posture,** so that you are back in *Pure Presence* and avoiding the pitfalls of emotional triggering.

STEP SIX: *Be responsive without interjecting*. Do not probe, ask questions, or interrupt. Your eyes, facial muscles, smile, nodding, eyebrow movements, and short responses, such as "Thanks," "Really?", "Aha," and so forth, will allow the other person you are speaking with to process their beta-alpha overlap and go on to discernment. With the practice of BE you will come to understand why many conversations self-destruct, and why we become easily distracted. It is when we enter back into our *ego state,* or become self-focused, that we derail the communication, and this leaves both parties feeling unheard and not valued.

STEP SEVEN: Respect and **welcome the silence** between the verbal communications. In this special time of stillness, we can catch a glimpse of our subconscious triggers and gain awareness of how and why we may choose to transform them. This can alter a belief, or worldview, we hold in our thinking brain, **allowing emotional shifting** and **behavioral re-direction to take place**.

STEP EIGHT: *Be patient*—with yourself and the other person—during the Behavioral Engagement process. The health professionals who use BE spend upward to an hour with each person they interview. It takes an unfolding of the other person's conversational comfort level, as well as trust in the *intention* of the exchange, for them to experience the *expansiveness* that Behavioral Engagement provides. Many of us are not used to being treated with such respect and integrity or experiencing such freedom to express our true thoughts and feelings.

It can take time for people to realize you do not have an agenda, or want a particular outcome from the exchange with them, and that you are not going to judge them or give advice or suggestions. Let's face it, many times we do.

STEP NINE: *Your intention will become your agenda*, so be honest with yourself about what your motive is for entering into the conversation. As you apply BE in your work and life, you will become more centered and less self-serving in your relationships. This *Pure Presence* intention will perfect your BE skills to strengthen and uplift all of your relationships and communications.

STEP TEN: At some point in the conversation you will verbally respond to the other person, and it is important that you **use "I" statements to express your feelings.** Using "I" statements shows that these are *your* feelings and not a statement about what occurred in a previous situation or discussion. To keep the emotional triggers, or *charge,* out of the conversation, we must own what *we* feel and not project our feelings as being the same for the other person. We must avoid trying to prove what we feel is *the truth*. In this appropriate way we show respect for the other person's experience, which is essential in the BE process.

STEP ELEVEN: *Allow for discovery*. One of the transformational components of BE is that if you remain true to the model and stay in your *Pure Presence* center, you will make discoveries that *will shift you emotionally*. These emotional shifts will bring about behavioral change in *you*, as well as reciprocal changes in the other person in the relationship. As we have learned, many behaviors are rooted in feelings and beliefs. When they shift, our behaviors can shift, and then we have sustainable, authentic behavioral change that can have positive long-term results in our lives and with our relationships.

STEP TWELVE: *Keep trying, and do not give up* on your skills development. Once you are exposed to BE, and experience the transformational power it has for yourself and your relationships, you will want to perfect it. Even if you have some frustrating experiences, lose your center, and *mind wander* during a conversation, you can start over again with the *next* conversation. The important thing is committing to improve the quality of communication in your relationships. In a short period of time you will become quite skilled as you experience a new level of success and fulfillment in *all* your relationships!

Food for Thought

"Even the rich are hungry for love, for being cared for, for being wanted, for having someone to call their own."
—Mother Teresa

Research and statistics demonstrate that relationships are critical to our health, happiness, and longevity. Published studies note that people who are in significant relationships live longer than people who are not. Men who are married live longer than men who are not. Men and women who have friends are more fulfilled than those who do not. Individuals who regularly attend a church or a community group are healthier than those who do not. Those who have pets are not as lonely as those who do not have them, and loneliness is the major cause of depression in the United States. Relationships: we want them and need them. Learning how to have better relationships is as much a part of staying healthy as eating good food, getting enough sleep, and exercising regularly.

Relationships—Let them Flow

"The best way to find yourself is to lose yourself in the service of others."
—Mahatma Gandhi

Our relationships are gifts: we can open and put them aside, or we can enjoy them and appreciate their life-enriching value. When we are young, many of us think that relationships are plentiful and that if things do not go well, we can easily replace one person with another. We often lose our friendships or intimate relationships because we *want more* out of a relationship or because of ego conflicts. Many of us learn later on that it is *giving more* to a relationship, rather than wanting more out of it, that makes a relationship successful.

Many years ago I heard someone ask, *"Would you rather be loved or be right?"* I took that to mean that if we want to be in relationships with others, it is important to understand that after survival, the human priority is to belong, to be loved rather than to be right or in control. We want and need nourishing and loving companionship. I sincerely hope this book has invited, and better enabled you, to have more fulfilling and successful relationships.

In the upcoming Part II we take a look at statistics on behaviors and explore the connection between our culture, relationships, and health.

(1) From your relationship experiences, which components of Behavioral Engagement were the easiest for you to relate to, and why? Which components offer a new perspective on how you may want to re-direct your relationship behaviors?

(2) Has the information in the last two chapters helped clarify for you why many of us struggle to change our behaviors?

(3) Identify some examples of times you have addressed ways to change your own behaviors and been successful in doing so. What do you think helped or hurt your ability to make these behavioral changes?

(4) If you have not experienced success in changing a particular behavior, was there anything you learned about behaviors from that experience that has helped you in other ways?

(5) What issues do you think are deterrents in making health-behavior changes or changes to your personal relationships?

(6) How has the information in this chapter motivated you to change your approach to relationship communication?

(7) Do you think this information would be helpful if you shared it with others with whom you have relationships?

Changing Behavior

PART II

Part II, Chapter Three
Behavior Data and Statistics

"We would rather be ruined than changed."
—W. H. Auden

Even a casual look at the leading problematic behaviors such as overeating, alcoholism, and drug use tells the story of increasing numbers of individuals dealing with relationship problems and health issues that are the direct result of behavioral choices. The numbers of both children and adult populations struggling with a variety of negative behaviors have significantly increased since the mid- to late 1980s. These trends indicate the degree of distress and the loss of control we are experiencing as a culture—a trend that is troubling for both the individual and our society as a whole.

This chapter lists statistics from the U.S. Centers for Disease Control and other reporting agencies on the top behaviors deemed detrimental to individuals, their relationships, and society in general.[1] I invite you to take a serious look at these statistics, charts, and graphs, as they will give you an appreciation for how we, as a collective society, are struggling with behavioral issues that directly or indirectly impact all of us.

Food and Behavior

The number-one detrimental health behavior today is related to food intake. Excessive body weight, morbid obesity, anorexia, and bulimia are differing aspects of what constitute *eating disorders*. Unhealthful eating and poor nutritional habits are believed to be one of the major causes of the leading chronic health conditions and the three major causes of death in the United States—heart disease, cancer, and stroke.

The statistics for these disorders are staggering and continue to grow each year. From the years 1991 through 2003, obesity rates in America went from an average of 11.9% to 23.5%, which represents a doubling in twelve years or a 1% increase each year.[2]

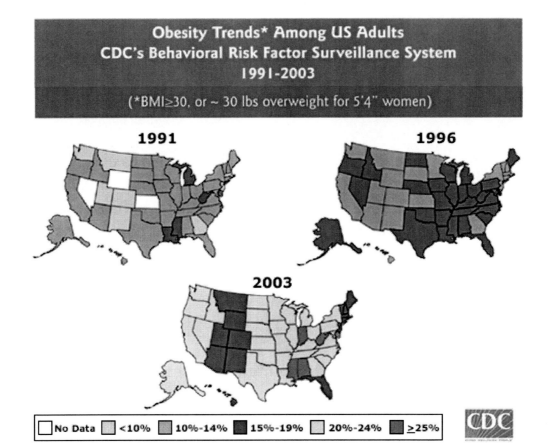

Obesity Trends* Among US Adults
CDC's Behavioral Risk Factor Surveillance System
1991-2003

(*BMI≥30, or ~ 30 lbs overweight for 5'4" women)

1991   1996

2003

No Data | <10% | 10%-14% | 15%-19% | 20%-24% | ≥25%

CDC

In 2006, only Mississippi had obesity rates of more than 30%. The CDC chart below, which brings us through 2006, shows the fifteen-year, 15% obesity increase across the country, continuing the 1% point increase per year.

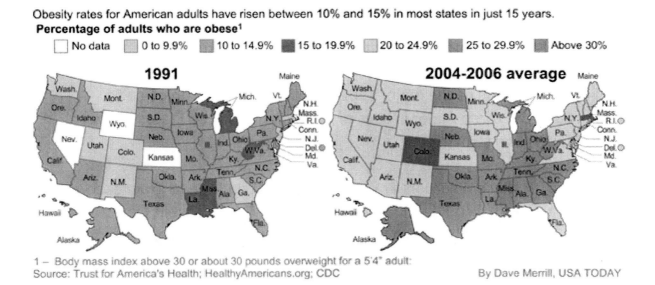

Obesity rates for American adults have risen between 10% and 15% in most states in just 15 years.
Percentage of adults who are obese[1]

No data | 0 to 9.9% | 10 to 14.9% | 15 to 19.9% | 20 to 24.9% | 25 to 29.9% | Above 30%

1991   2004-2006 average

1 – Body mass index above 30 or about 30 pounds overweight for a 5'4" adult:
Source: Trust for America's Health; HealthyAmericans.org; CDC

By Dave Merrill, USA TODAY

In 2009, nine states had adult obesity rates greater than 30%:

Mississippi—33.8%	Alabama—31.6%
Tennessee—31.6%	West Virginia—31.3%
Louisiana—31.2%	Oklahoma—30.6%
Kentucky—30.5%	Arkansas—30.1%

and Missouri—30%

For six straight years, Mississippi led the country in adult obesity, at 33.8%. Michigan was the only non-southern state to score in the top ten for obesity rate, tied with North Carolina for the tenth spot, a 29.4% obesity rate.

In 2009, Colorado topped the list of the "thinnest" states, with an adult obesity rate of only 16.9%. "Skinny" states include Hawaii 18.2%, Massachusetts 18.6%, Rhode Island 19.5%, and Montana 19.9% http://www.cdc.gov/obesity/data/trends.html.

Obesity rates for American children were even grimmer, with a percentage rate for Mexican-American males rapidly approaching the 50% mark.[3] These statistics are retrieved from the Centers for Disease Control databases and are consistently accurate and predicative.

For American children ages 2–19 in 2009 the following percentages are classified as overweight or obese, using the 95th percentile or higher of body mass index (BMI) values on the CDC growth chart:
> **For non-Hispanic whites, 31.9% of males and 29.5% of females**
> **For non-Hispanic blacks, 30.8% of males and 39.2% of females**

Excess eating can develop as a coping mechanism to reduce anxiety or emotional pain and to enhance pleasure. These coping mechanisms and behaviors are passed on to our children, potentially creating serious health problems for them, as well as establishing lifelong patterns for their nutrition and eating behaviors.

Projections

The final chart, shown below, is the calculation of adult obesity for 2012, based on previous statistics. **The projected obesity and overweight percentiles for adult Americans over the age of twenty years old in 2012 are a combined 68%.**

2012 Projections for American Adults 20 and Up

Obesity is defined as a BMI of 30 or greater.

Rankings were computed by CalorieLab based on a three-year average of state-by-state statistics for adult Obesity Percentages from the Centers for Disease Control's (CDC) Behavioral Risk Factor Surveillance System database.

- Percent of adults age 20 years and over who are obese: 34% (2011–2012)
- Percent of adults age 20 years and over who are overweight (and not obese): 34% (2011–2012)

Looking at the Numbers

It is unlikely that anyone could look at these numbers, calculated and published by the U.S. Centers for Disease Control, and not ask the obvious question of why so many Americans are exhibiting out-of-control eating behaviors.

What, when, and how we eat is one of the few remaining behaviors over which we can exert control. Eating is a physical, biochemical, social, emotional, environmental, cultural, and for some, spiritual activity that we can participate in anywhere, at any time of the day or night, alone or with a group of people. Considering the current projection that 68% of Americans, or two out of every three of us, are overweight or obese, can there be any question that the United States is in the grip of some form of eating behavior disorder? Keep in mind these figures do not factor in the statistics for other eating disorders, such as anorexia, bulimia, or over exercising and dieting to the point of obsession.

Problems with both obesity and excess body weight are now so out of control that a suggestion was made by a well-respected Harvard physician in the July 13, 2011, *Journal of the American Medical Association* that morbidly obese children be taken from their parents if the feeding and eating conditions in the home do not improve. Additionally, insurance companies and employers are discussing the possibility of fines and penalties for morbidly obese adults.[4] What has caused our obesity rate to go from 11% in the late 1980s to the 2012 projection of 34% in this short period of time?

Many experts point to the lack of exercise and a sedentary lifestyle, as well as fast-food consumption and less nutritious foods. But are these really the causes of such a wide-scale change in our nation's behavior and health? Or are we using food as a means to crank up our *feel-good* hormones and the neurotransmitters that affect our brain function and mood? Are we self-medicating with food to mask feelings of anxiety, emotional pain, or other issues? Is there a way to stop the cycle of pain and self-medication? Is there a way to address this?

Behavioral Engagement, the behavioral change model that is the subject of this book, has demonstrated in numerous pilot studies that a *whole-person* approach to changing behavior is necessary to facilitate a *sustained* shift in an individual's unhealthful or self-destructive behavior. Behavioral change models must address what causes the behavior, not just the presenting symptoms of the behavior. Behavioral Engagement focuses on creating an environment that invites a shift of the individual's worldview. This shifting of perspective is critically important for sustainable change to occur and to further prevent unconscious, underlying emotions or problematic behaviors from being re-triggered by the *reactive mind*.

Alcohol, Tobacco, and Drug Behaviors

The headlines and statistics surrounding the widespread and excessive use of alcohol, tobacco, and drugs—both legal and illegal—is something we have become all too familiar with.

The evening news feeds us a continuous stream of coverage and facts on these subjects, to the point where many of us have tuned out. By now, we are all consciously aware of the implications of alcohol excess and abuse, the dangers of smoking, unhealthful eating habits, lack of exercise, and other behaviors that can lead to not only early death and disease, but also crime and violence.

It appears, however, that unless we are directly impacted by these health-risk behaviors, or someone we care about is, we do not realize the extent of the harm they have on the individuals who ultimately become the statistics, or the victims, of these behaviors. Listed below is a quick overview of some of the top behavior-driven statistics.[5]

In the United States, in 2009, 59% of all death for adults older than 25 years of age were related to six categories of health-risk behaviors that resulted in cardiovascular or cancer deaths: (1) tobacco use (2) alcohol and other drug use; (3) sexual behaviors that contribute to STDs, including human immunodeficiency virus (HIV) infection as well as unwanted pregnancy; (4) unhealthy dietary behaviors; (5) physical inactivity; (6) behaviors that contribute to unintentional injuries or violence.

Health-risk behavior studies developed by the CDC identify these behaviors as being frequently interrelated and established during childhood and adolescence. These behaviors then extend into adulthood.

Read the report at
http://www.cdc.gov/mmwr/preview/mmwrhtml/ss5905a1.htm.
http://www.cdc.gov/yrbs.

Tobacco Use

In 2010, the use of tobacco and smoking still remained the leading preventable cause of disease, disability, and death in the United States. Between 1964 and 2004, cigarette smoking caused an estimated 12 million deaths, including 4.1 million deaths from cancer and 5.5 million deaths from cardiovascular diseases.[6]

Thirty percent of all U.S. cancers are related to tobacco. It is estimated that directly or indirectly, nearly 20% of all U.S. deaths annually are attributed to the use of tobacco. This translates to 400,000 deaths per year.
http://www.acde.org/common/Tobacco.htm

There are fifteen tobacco-related types of cancer. The World Health Organization estimates that every year 5.4 million premature deaths occur globally as a result of the use of tobacco.[7] And yet we keep smoking, just as we keep eating. Smoking is a self-soothing behavior that stimulates the opiate-like chemicals our bodies produce naturally to reduce anxiety.

Just as with eating, we have the choice to smoke anytime by ourselves or with others. Overeating and smoking are two behaviors that generally do not require anyone's permission. The biochemistry of increased dopamine and serotonin from both of those behaviors helps us, in the short term, feel less anxious or hopeless. And there is the social aspect to both behaviors as well.

In 2010, these rates have changed only slightly, with one out of five American deaths attributable to tobacco. In addition, currently 8.6 million people in the United States suffer from chronic conditions such as bronchitis, emphysema and cardiovascular disease. Currently 23% of U.S. adults and 30% of adolescents smoke, for a combined total of 47 million smokers; 70.3 million Americans use tobacco products.

With alcohol, the latest numbers look like this:[8]

> Excessive alcohol use is the third leading cause of death in the United States.

> Each year 79,000 deaths are attributed to excessive alcohol use in the United States.

> Excessive alcohol use is responsible for 2.3 million years of potential life lost annually—an average of thirty years of potential life lost for each death.

> In 2005 more than 1.6 million hospitalizations and more than 4 million emergency room visits were for alcohol-related conditions.

> 52% of adults aged eighteen and up are current, regular drinkers.

Alcohol is one of the most widely used substances in the world. Alcohol use and binge drinking among Americans is a serious health problem. Binge drinking is defined as four (4) or more drinks within one to several hours for women, and five (5) or more drinks within one to several hours for men.

It has been determined that most people who binge-drink are not alcoholics or alcohol dependent. Excessive alcohol use, which is often the direct result of binge drinking, can result in serious behavioral and health risks.

Binge drinking, like tobacco use and overeating behaviors, is usually triggered by an emotional or social situation. Our desire to belong and fit in, daily stress or anxiety, as well as our interactions within unhealthy family or personal relationships can set off a binge-drinking episode as an attempt to self-soothe the feelings of pain or fear we may experience but not express.

The CDC in their Alcohol Fact Sheet lists the risks of binge drinking and the potential outcomes:[9]

http://www.cdc.gov/alcohol/fact-sheets/alcohol-use.htm

- Unintentional injuries, including traffic injuries, falls, drowning, burns, and unintentional firearm injuries.

- Violence, including intimate partner violence and child maltreatment. About 35% of victims report that offenders are under the influence of alcohol. Alcohol use is associated with two out of three incidents of intimate partner violence.

- Studies have also shown that alcohol is a leading factor in child maltreatment and neglect cases and is the most frequent substance abused by these parents.

- Risky sexual behaviors, including unprotected sex, sex with multiple partners, and increased risk of sexual assault. These behaviors can result in unintended pregnancy or sexually transmitted diseases.

- Miscarriage and stillbirth among pregnant women and a combination of physical and mental birth defects among children that last throughout life.

- Alcohol poisoning, a medical emergency that results from high blood-alcohol levels that suppress the central nervous system and can cause loss of consciousness, low blood pressure and body temperature, coma, respiratory depression, or death.

- Alcohol is also now being correlated with forms of early onset dementia and reduced cognitive function.

Long-Term Health Risks of Alcohol[10]

Over time, excessive alcohol use can lead to the development of chronic diseases, neurological impairments, and social problems, including but not limited to the list found below.

- Neurological problems, including dementia, stroke, and neuropathy

- Cardiovascular problems, including myocardial infarction, cardiomyopathy, atrial fibrillation, and hypertension

- Psychiatric problems, including depression, anxiety, and suicide

- Social problems, including unemployment, lost productivity, and family problems

- Cancer of the mouth, throat, esophagus, liver, colon, and breast. In general, the risk of cancer increases with increasing amounts of alcohol.
  Liver diseases, including the following:

- Alcoholic hepatitis

- Cirrhosis, which is among the fifteen leading causes of all deaths in the U.S.

- Among people with Hepatitis C virus, worsening of liver function and interference with medications used to treat this condition

- Other gastrointestinal problems, including pancreatitis and gastritis

For the full report refer to http://www.cdc.gov/alcohol/fact-sheets/alcohol-use.htm. For in-depth statistics visit
http://www.cancer.org/acs/groups/content/@epidemiologysurveilance/documents/document/acspc-026238.pdf
http://www.cdc.gov/nchs/data/series/sr_10/sr10_249.pdf smoking; pg 96; table 25 / alcohol pg 19; tables 26–27 pgs 98–99
http://www.cdc.gov/alcohol/publications.htm.
Centers for Disease Control and Prevention (CDC). *Alcohol-Related Disease Impact (ARDI)*. Atlanta, GA: CDC. Available at
http://www.cdc.gov/alcohol/ardi.htm. March 28, 2008.

Drug Use

GRAPH OF ILLICIT DRUG USE 2002–2009

A total of16.7 million Americans aged twelve and older reporting past-month use in 2009. A 6.6% increase in usage—the highest in eight years—drove up overall illicit drug use.

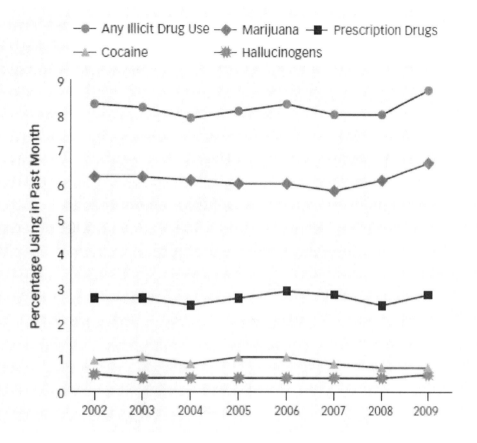

The comprehensive report can be found at http://www.nida.nih.gov/NIDA_notes/NNvol23N3/tearoff.html.

Statistics from 2009 from the National Institute of Drug Abuse, the National Institutes of Health, provide us with the most current profile on drug use and abuse in the United States.[11]

> ➤ Illicit drug use in the United States has risen to its highest level in eight years, according to the 2009 National Survey on Drug Use and Health. In 2009, 8.7% of Americans aged twelve and older—an estimated 21.8 million people—said they used illicit drugs in the month before the survey, which represents a 9% increase over the 2008 rate.

➢ Abuse of prescription drugs, and the less frequently used methamphetamine and ecstasy, also saw increases. Nonmedical use of prescription drugs rose 12%, from 2.5% in 2008 to 2.8% in 2009. Abuse of methamphetamine rose from 0.1% to 0.2%, and ecstasy from 0.2% to 0.3%.

➢ Alcohol in combination with other drugs was the most frequently mentioned drug at time of emergency department admission (204,524), followed by cocaine (174,896), heroin/morphine (97,287), and marijuana (96,446).

The 2009 survey also found the following:[12]

• Drug abuse among those aged fifty to fifty-nine doubled to 6.2% from 2.7% in 2002. This trend reflects the entry into this age bracket of increasing numbers of baby boomers, who have a higher rate of illicit drug use than older cohorts.

• Only about 11% of those who need treatment for drug or alcohol abuse received therapy in a specialty facility. Previous years showed a similar disparity.

The annual NSDUH survey is sponsored by SAMHSA. The 2009 results are based on responses from 68,700 civilians nationwide who do not live in institutions. The report is available online at www.oas.samhsa.gov/NSDUH/2k9NSDUH/2k9Results.htm. SOURCE: Substance Abuse and Mental Health Services Administration, 2010. *Results from the 2009 National Survey on Drug Use and Health: Volume I. Summary of National Findings* (Office of Applied Studies, NSDUH Series H-38A, HHS Publication No. SMA 10-4586). Rockville, MD. [Full Text] http://www.usnodrugs.com/drug-addiction-statistics.htm

"What's going on here?"

After reading these startling statistics, gathered and reported by reliable sources, any rational person would ask the question, *"What is going on in our society?"* We have just looked at four common behaviors that most of us are familiar with, yet there are dozens of others. Among them are intimate partner violence (IPV), also referred to as domestic violence or domestic abuse, and the unimaginable neglect and abuse of children.

Intimate Partner Violence

http://www.cdc.gov/violenceprevention/pdf/IPV_factsheet-a.pdf

IPV is a serious problem in the United States.[13]

- Each year women experience about 4.8 million intimate partner–related physical assaults and rapes. Men are the victims of about 2.9 million intimate partner–related physical assaults.

- IPV resulted in 2,340 deaths in 2007. Of these deaths, 70% were females and 30% were males.

- The medical care, mental health services, and lost productivity (e.g., time away from work) cost of IPV was an estimated $5.8 billion in 1995. Updated to 2003 dollars, that's more than $8.3 billion.

Several factors can increase the risk that someone will hurt his or her partner. Having these risk factors does not mean that IPV will occur.

Risk factors for perpetration (hurting a partner):

- **Being violent or aggressive in the past**
- **Seeing or being a victim of violence as a child**
- **Using drugs or alcohol, especially drinking heavily**
- **Not having a job or other life events that cause stress**

A report by the national Network to End Domestic Violence (NNEDM) identifies the influence of economical stress and DPV:
http://dvam.vawnet.org/docs/materials/09-resource-packet/Issue_FactsSheets_Handouts/ImpactofEconomy_FactSheet.pdf

THE IMPACT OF THE ECONOMY ON DOMESTIC VIOLENCE

Although an economic downturn itself does not cause domestic violence, it can exacerbate the factors that contribute to domestic violence and reduce victims' ability to flee.[14]

- Domestic violence is more than three times as likely to occur when couples are experiencing high levels of financial strain as when they are experiencing low levels of financial strain.

- Women whose male partners experienced two or more periods of unemployment over a five-year study were almost three times as likely to be victims of intimate partner violence as women whose partners were in stable jobs.

- Victims frequently report economic needs: in one study, 93% of victims requested help with economic issues and 61% needed three or more of five kinds of economic help offered.

- Seventy-three percent of shelters attributed the rise in abuse to "financial issues." "Stress" and "job loss" (61% and 49%, respectively) were also frequently cited as causing the rise in the number of victims seeking shelter.

- Three out of four domestic violence shelters report an increase in women seeking assistance from abuse since September 2008.

- The region with the largest reported increase in women seeking help as a result of domestic violence was the South (78%), followed by the Midwest (74%), the Northeast (72%), and the West (71%).

This report circles us back to the discussion in Chapter 1, which focused on our survival imperatives and how our survival can feel threatened in various ways. We respond to this threat in the way our sensory motor *imprints* have conditioned us to. For many of us, our response can be one of hostility and even violence.

The Emotional and Physical Abuse of Children

Neglect and the emotional and physical abuse of children are most often perpetuated by individuals who were themselves abused in this way. Here are the heartbreaking statistics on the emotional and physical violence that is enacted upon children.[15]

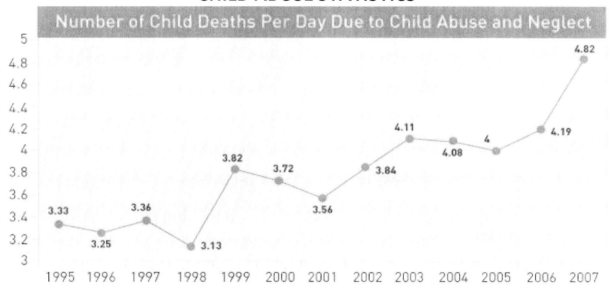

CHILD ABUSE STATISTICS

"Children are suffering from a hidden epidemic of child abuse and neglect. Over 3 million reports of child abuse are made every year in the United States; however, those reports can include multiple children. In 2009, approximately 3.3 million child abuse reports and allegations were made involving an estimated 6 million children."

http://www.childwelfare.gov/pubs/factsheets/long_term_consequences.cfm

When we hear about child abuse, we generally think of children being *sexually* abused. Sexual abuse of children is a heinous, criminal offense, punishable by law. People who enact the sexual abuse of children are viewed as deviant and abnormal. This behavior is considered so heinous and destructive that even within prison populations these individuals are shunned or often killed.

Although sexual abuse tragically does occur in 9.1% of child abuse cases, physical abuse, psychological abuse, medical neglect, and other forms of abuse occur the majority, or 91.9%, of the time.

There were 3.3 million abuse cases reported in 2008, which involved 6 million children. Of those cases 772,000 were substantiated. There was a 1.1% increase in reported childhood abuse cases in 2008, compared with cases reported in 2007.

When most of us think of child abusers, we imagine a monster victimizing the most vulnerable among us. We associate child abuse with mentally imbalanced, malevolent males harming young victims. The shocking statistics about child abuse is that it is most often *a child's mother* who is the abuser.

A report of child abuse is made every ten seconds.

- **Almost five children die every day as a result of child abuse. More than three out of four are under the age of four.**
- **It is estimated that between 60% and 85% of child fatalities caused by maltreatment are not recorded as such on death certificates.**
- **90% of child sexual abuse victims know the perpetrator in some way; 68% are abused by family members.**
- **Child abuse occurs at every socioeconomic level, across ethnic and cultural lines, within all religions, and at all levels of education.**
- **About 30% of abused and neglected children will later abuse their own children, continuing the horrible cycle of abuse.**

These children were neglected or abused by their parents 81.1% of the time and by their extended families 6.5% of the time. Women abuse children more frequently than men do, as confirmed by the stunning statistic that the *child's biological mother* is the most frequent abuser.[16]

A comprehensive report can be found at http://www.acf.hhs.gov/programs/cb/pubs/cm08/cm08.pdf.

Statistics for child abuse are shocking. We want to believe that the people abusing children must be from fringe communities in our society. But they are not. Child abuse occurs across all strata of society—rich, poor, educated, uneducated, skilled, and unskilled. Child abuse occurs in every state in the country and in all neighborhoods regardless of status or affluence.

Many forms of child abuse are not visible, such as emotional and psychological abuse that cannot often be demonstrated or proven. Parents who appear in all other ways healthy and productive members of their community can either intentionally or unconsciously abuse their children. The frequency of child abuse is believed to be significantly greater than available statistics, as so much of it is not easily identified or proven, such as emotional abuse, and therefore not reported.

What drives someone to physically neglect or emotionally abuse a child? Data shows that one out of three abused children will go on to abuse their own children and continue the cycle. What must be going on emotionally or psychologically for the parent who neglects or physically harms their child?

Studies confirm that violence and physical or emotional abuse is the acting out of rage, anger, shame, or feelings of loss of control. This acting out can lead to the emotional or physical abuse of another person. Those who abuse others have most often been abused themselves. They have learned to relieve their overwhelmed emotional states through this destructive coping behavior.

The secondary effects of child abuse results in elevated rates of criminal behavior. United States government statistics show that 14% of all men in prison were reported to have been abused as children, and 36% of all women in prison were abused.

In addition, children who experience child abuse and neglect are 59% more likely to be arrested as a juvenile, 28% more likely to be arrested as an adult, and 30% more likely to commit violent crime.

http://www.childwelfare.gov/pubs/factsheets/long_term_consequences.cfm
http://www.acf.hhs.gov/programs/cb
http://www.childhelp.org/pages/statistics

The Big Picture of Human Behavior

Definition of *BEHAVIOR*
— **be·hav·ior·** \bi-hā-vyər, bē-\ noun

a: the manner of conducting oneself *b:* anything that an organism does involving action and response to stimulation *c:* the response of an individual, group, or species to its environment

The expression *"Actions speak louder than words"* means our behaviors demonstrate our true feelings or intentions more accurately than our words do.

It is widely accepted by mental health, medical, and law enforcement professionals that behaviors, as they are defined in Merriam-Webster Online, are *responses to stimulation or our response to the environment.*

The behaviors we have looked at in this chapter are to a lesser or greater degree self-soothing, adaptive behaviors. It is our attempt to reduce painful emotional responses to *triggering stimuli*, which may come from the environment or directly from another person. Lighting up a cigarette, binge drinking or eating, or verbal, emotional, or physical abuse toward others make up a continuum of behaviors that express the degree to which we are either acting out or self-medicating the hurt of imprinted pain.

Although these are innate mechanisms for survival or coping, they are destructive for us and to others; therefore, making sustainable changes to these and other behaviors are an acknowledged challenge. Many variables affect whether or not an individual can make behavioral changes and how long those behaviors can be re-directed before a primal trigger will occur and derail the effort.

This chapter has contained startling information about significant behavior problems in our culture. The real surprise, however, is how *all* of these behaviors, no matter how seemingly moderate or severe, have their roots in our brains' imperative to *avoid pain and seek pleasure.*

The relationship between our relationships, behavior, and health, as well as a look at the impact culture and environment play in behavior, will be further explored in the next chapter. This information will lay a foundation to better understand how we can make sustainable changes to our behaviors and within our relationships.

Other chronic self-destructive behaviors include the following:

Gambling—Research reveals that in America, approximately 2.5 million adults suffer from compulsive gambling, about 3 million are considered problem gamblers, around 15 million adults are under the risk of becoming problem gamblers, and 148 million fall under the low-risk gambler category.[17]
http://rehab-international.org/gambling-addiction/gambling-addiction-statistics

Compulsive Shopping—Lorrin Koran, MD, researcher at Stanford University, in 2006 published a study with his colleagues in the *American Journal of Psychiatry* with more than 2,500 subjects. The study concluded that compulsive overspending or overshopping affects approximately 6% of the U.S. population, or 17 million people, with equal amounts of men and women. Other surveys estimate 2%–12%.[18] http://ajp.psychiatryonline.org/cgi/content/abstract/163/10/1806

Hoarding—More than 6 million people, or one out of twenty, in the United States hoard. It is calculated that "2%–5% of Americans may meet the criteria for being hoarders," says David Tolin, PhD, a hoarding expert and author of *Buried in Treasures.*[19] http://www.webmd.com/mental-health/features/harmless-pack-rat-or-compulsive-hoarder?page=2

Nonsuicidal Injurious Behavior—Research addressing the epidemiology and phenomenology of nonsuicidal self-injury (NSSI) among adolescents appears in articles of *Medline* and *Psychinfo*. Findings indicate a lifetime prevalence of NSSI ranging from 13.0% to 23.2%. Reasons for engaging in NSSI are reported as regulating emotions and may be attempts to elicit attention.[20]
http://www.ncbi.nlm.nih.gov/pubmed/17453692/

Infidelity—30% to 60% of all married individuals in the United States will engage in infidelity behaviors sometime during their marriage. These statistics come from research by David Bush and Todd Shackleford at the University of Texas.[21]
http://homepage.psy.utexas.edu/homepage/Group/BussLAB/pdffiles/susceptibility%20to%20infidelity-jrp-1997.pdf

This is just a partial list of behaviors that many of us engage in. Currently, the study of human behaviors and attempts to identify solutions to assist in transforming these behaviors is a key area of focus for social scientists.

(1) Which behavior statistics were the most surprising to you? Have you had experience with any of these behaviors yourself?

(2) Has the information in the last two chapters helped clarify for you why many of us struggle to change our behaviors?

(3) Have you spent time addressing ways to change your own behaviors and been successful in doing so? What do you think helped or hurt your ability to make these behavioral changes?

(4) If you have not experienced success in changing a particular behavior, was there anything you learned about behaviors from that experience that has helped you in other ways?

(5) What issues do you think are deterrents in making health-behavior changes or changes to your personal relationships?

(6) Did the information in this chapter motivate you to make any new behavioral changes?

(7) Do you think this information would be helpful or worthwhile for you to share with others?

In the closing chapter we will explore cultural and environmental impacts on our relationships and health.

Part II, Chapter Four
Relationships, Culture, and Health

"We are never so hopelessly unhappy as when we lose love."
—Sigmund Freud, MD

The quality of our relationships and our health are intimately connected. Ample research today evidences and reveals how our relationships with family members, pets, and even houseplants can affect our health in a positive way. By the same token, if our relationships create ongoing stress or prolonged conflict, we are more likely to become ill.

The widely published Harvard Mastery of Stress study that began in the 1950s studied 126 male Harvard undergraduates to identify which factors would help them deal with stress and develop resilience.[1] As part of the study all the participants had been asked to rate how much they felt their parents loved and cared for them while they were growing up.

Thirty-five years later a husband-and-wife team of Harvard researchers, Linda Russek, PhD, and Gary E. Schwartz, PhD, revisited the outcomes of the study, which had been used for medical and psychological research. Russek and Schwartz focused on twenty-eight questions within the study to assess if these simple ratings of perceived parental love recorded in the early 1950s might serve as predictors of the men's health thirty-five years later in 1993.[2]

With the help of computer analysis the researchers compared the subjects' responses in the 1950s with their state of health in 1993. The data was analyzed and fell into three categories based on the information the subjects had given about their parents:

- Of those men who rated both parents high in love and caring, only 25% had been diagnosed with some form of serious illness by 1993. The diseases included heart problems, high blood pressure, arthritis, heart disease, and asthma.

- Of those who rated one parent high in love and caring and one parent low in loving and caring, 50% had been diagnosed with some form of serious illness by 1993.

- Of those who rated both parents low in terms of love and caring, 87% had been diagnosed with some form of serious illness by 1993.

The researchers found that these patterns of health were independent of family and genetic history of disease. They were independent of the death and divorce history of parents. They were also independent of the smoking and marital history of the men themselves. None of these familiar, long-established risk factors could explain the findings. What is important about the outcomes analysis is that they were not related to any other identifiable factor *except* for the perception of love and caring provided by the subjects' parents.

While medicine has attempted to established clear risk factors and definable behaviors with predictable outcomes, the field of social psychology and epidemiology has also identified the powerful effects our feelings and emotions have on our health and wellness.

Susan A. Everson, an epidemiologist at the Western Consortium for Public Health in Berkeley, California, and her colleagues, including epidemiologist George A. Kaplan of the California Department of Health Services in Berkeley, a coauthor of a report on a Finland study, say that *"It looks like people who experience a pervasive sense of hopelessness are at increased risk for a variety of serious health problems."*[3]

The study consisted of 2,428 men age forty-two to sixty, living in Finland and participating in an ongoing study of psychological contributions to cardiovascular disease. The hopelessness of the study participants was rated by their response to questions about their current state of hopefulness or hopelessness.

Of the study participants, those who reported moderate to high hopelessness died from all recorded causes at two to three times the rate of those reporting low or no hopelessness. Everson's group also reported that the most hopeless group of participants also developed cancer and experienced heart attacks more frequently. Michael F. Scheier, a psychologist at Carnegie Mellon University in Pittsburgh, says, *"Much previous research indicates that optimism in the face of losses and failures promotes mental and physical health, whereas pessimism does the reverse."*[4]

More research on the connections between relationships and health were reported in the June 25, 1997, *Journal of the American Medical Association.*[5] Psychologist Sheldon Cohen, of Carnegie Mellon University in Pittsburgh, and his coworkers published a study that consisted of 125 men and 151 women. Ranging in age from eighteen to fifty-five, they were all in good physical health.

These volunteers began the study by reporting their amount of interactions with other people, including spouses, parents, children, friends, coworkers, and members of various volunteer and religious groups. In the second phase each participant received nasal drops containing a cold virus. Over the next five days participants were housed individually and allowed to interact with each other only at a distance of at least three (3) feet apart.

Within those five days, the investigators reported that the signs of a viral infection and cold symptoms rose sharply among those who had reported the lowest number of social relationships. This pattern held regardless of age, sex, race, amount of education, or the season in which the trials were held.

The report also said that sleep problems, alcohol abstinence, low vitamin C intake, or cigarette smoking, as well as being socially introverted, were only *partially* accountable for the number of colds found in the socially restricted subjects.

Relationships and health are not limited to our human connections. A study by researcher Dr. Karen Allen, at the State University of New York at Buffalo, identified that individuals who suffered from hypertension had lower blood pressure readings during stressful situations after adopting a dog or cat than their counterparts who did not have a pet companion.[6]

There are even studies about how having a relationship with houseplants can affect health. Dr. Ellen Langer, a professor in the psychology department at Harvard University, reports on that phenomenon in her book *Counter Clockwise:*

In the 1970s my colleague Judith Rodin and I conducted an experiment with nursing home residents. We encouraged one group of participants to find ways to make more decisions for themselves.

For example, they were allowed to choose where to receive visitors, and if and when to watch the movies that were shown at the home. Each also chose a houseplant to care for, and they were to decide where to place the plant in their room, as well as when and how much to water it.

A second, control group received no such instructions to make their own decisions; they were given houseplants but told that the nursing staff would care for them. A year and a half later, we found that members of the first group were more cheerful, active, and alert, based on a variety of tests we had administered both before and after the experiment.

Allowing for the fact that they were all elderly and quite frail at the start, we were pleased that they were also much healthier: we were surprised, however, that less than half as many of the more engaged group had died than had those in the control group.[7]

Building Better Relationships

We now know just how important relationships are to our health and fulfillment. We also know from our own personal experiences just how challenging these essential relationships can be. Many of us are puzzled about why the people we care about behave the way they do in relationship with us, and what if anything we can do about it. We are not alone. For many decades, psychologists, educators, criminologists, and medical professionals have been trying to crack the code on what causes individuals to behave as they do, and what specific factors influence an individual to change their behavior.

Identifying personality types to predict behavior is commonly used in law enforcement and jury profiling. It is also used to predict social behaviors. In health care, substantial research has been done on personality, health behaviors, and chronic disease, along with research on emotional states causing illness.

The real challenge has been to identify the *tipping point* in behavioral change that can predictably affect whether an individual makes self-directed changes in either their relationships or their health behaviors. In the field of psychology, behavioral change is addressed by a wide selection of personality and behavior models, behavioral theories, and practice models that explore this complex topic from a whole-person perspective. Currently, researchers are looking more closely at culture and environment as possible tipping points that impact behaviors.

The Impact of Culture and Environment

An interesting turn of events occurred in the United States during the mid-1980s that likely kick-started, or significantly contributed to, the health statistics we see in the late 1980s through early 1990s. Since that time, our obesity rates have climbed 1% a year to the current level of 34%. Given the bigger perspective we now have on our physical, emotional, nutritional, environmental, and even our spiritual or value-based needs, it is easy to imagine that a particular event, or even a series of events, created the *tipping point* leading to where we are today.

Life magazine reported the results of a 1980 reader survey that indicated that 80% of Americans were satisfied with their work, their appearance, and their quality of life.[8] Then—something unexpected happened—a cultural phenomenon occurred that shifted how a majority of us wanted to live our lives. In the fall of 1984, Robin Leach's *Lifestyles of the Rich and Famous* was aired for the first time on national television. It both shocked and seduced the American viewing audiences with stories of wealth and luxury beyond our wildest imagination.[9]

The well-kept secrets of the opulent and ostentatious lifestyles being lived outside our field of vision was suddenly thrust before us on prime-time television. We were now watching *the beautiful people* who were living the high life, materially enjoying everything money could buy. Although we had known that wealthy people lived differently from the rest of us, we had never seen it. We had no idea that they were living with such unrestrained abundance. Once we did, it fueled a desire and a drive to have at least some of that lifestyle for ourselves.

It no longer seemed enough to have a decent job, a nice house in the suburbs, and a two-week summer vacation. We wanted more, and we quickly thought of ways to get it. Suddenly, physical therapists and legal secretaries were leaving their careers to become commodity brokers or real estate developers. It was open season for anything that promised riches in a short period of time—that could provide us some of the luxury we saw each week in our middle-class living rooms.

We began taking loans for new cars and extravagant vacations. We used credit cards for the things we wanted. We went all out to claim a piece of this alluring dream. The late-1980s banking scandal slowed us down for a while, but with the advent of the dot-com boom we were back on the horse again, and riding hard. Technology and the Internet were also changing our lives in new ways.

We had to work harder and earn more, which meant multi-tasking and longer hours. To accommodate these changes our children spent less time playing and more time in organized activities. We were now eating the majority of our meals outside the home so we had the time to work longer hours to keep from falling behind or losing our sense of belonging to this new illusion of prosperity.

Let us fast-forward to 2010, when two Princeton University professors, Angus Deaton, the Dwight D. Eisenhower Professor of International Affairs and professor of economics and international affairs, and Daniel Kahneman, the Eugene Higgins Professor of Psychology and professor of psychology and public affairs (emeritus), analyzed more than 450,000 life-evaluation survey responses of randomly selected U.S. residents. They said, *"We conclude that lack of money (less than $75,000 income) brings both emotional misery and low life evaluation."*

"Similar results were found for anger," wrote the authors. *"Beyond $75,000 in the contemporary United States, however, higher income is neither the road to experienced happiness nor the road to the relief of unhappiness or stress, although higher income continues to improve an individual's life evaluations."*[10]

This income barometer is about **autonomy**—to self-govern, to have control over our life. Social scientists from the Victoria University of Wellington in New Zealand examined what was more important to well-being—having money or having autonomy. A large cohort group of 420,599 people, from sixty-three countries around the world, were followed for more than thirty years. They came from every social, financial, and political culture. The results of the study showed that regardless of where respondents lived, they tended to report greater well-being if they felt that they had autonomy. In environments where money did not impact an individual's autonomy there was no correlation with either happiness or *a better life.*[11]

Road Rage

Previously, we discussed the statistical explosion of eating-behavior shifts since the mid- to late 1980s, with obesity growing at a 1% rate per year since the late 1980s. Another current, escalating behavior we are all familiar with is road rage. It is often a topic of standup comedy, but road rage is no laughing matter.

In his congressional testimony to the Subcommittee on Surface Transportation and Infrastructure, U.S. House of Representatives (Washington, DC, July 17, 1997), Dr. Leon James, professor of traffic psychology, University of Hawaii, Honolulu, said this:

Road rage is a culturally acquired [behavior]. Road rage is becoming a major problem for motorists and high mileage company car drivers. 78% of company car drivers said that at some time another driver had verbally abused them, while 21% said that another driver had forced them to pull over or off the road.

However, although most cases of road rage did not lead to physical injury—only 3% suffered from physical violence—10% suffered damage to their car from road ragers. [The combination of] driving and habitual road rage has become virtually inseparable.

Professor James went on to say that we are in "*an epidemic of road rage*" and discusses his groundbreaking research of having drivers record their reactions while driving. Here are his comments about that experience:

The culture of road rage has deep roots. We inherit aggressive and dangerous driving patterns as children, watching our parents and other adults behind the wheel, and by watching and absorbing bad driving behaviors depicted in movies and television commercials.

I was astounded the first time I listened to drivers who had tape recorded their thoughts and feelings in traffic, speaking their thoughts aloud while driving, giving a sort of play-by-play of what it's like inside the private world of the driver.

This was the first time in the history of psychology that self-witnessing data became available through hundreds of drivers speaking and recording their thoughts in traffic. One feature that particularly amazed me was the pervasive negativity of their thoughts and feelings. In a kind of Jekyll and Hyde effect perfectly ordinary, friendly, good-hearted people tend to become extremely intolerant and anti-social as soon as they get behind the wheel.

Behind the wheel their personality undergoes a rapid transformation, from polite and tolerant to inconsiderate, intolerant and emotionally unintelligent.

As a result of my studies, I've concluded that aggressive drivers need other behavioral modification techniques to manage their competitive impulses on the road. I refer to this set of emotional management techniques as inner power tools for smart driving.

One of the most informative pieces of his testimony is his discussion of the cultural acceptance of road rage. In further explaining his years of research he provides an answer for why so many of us act out as we do on the road. He says the following:

It took several years of research for me to understand the psychological mechanism of emotionally impaired driving. The car is not only an object of convenience, beauty, and status. It is also a cultural and psychological object, associated with the driver's internal mental and emotional dynamics, our ego.

Cars are an extension of the self, they are ego-laden objects that can be used both positively and negatively to get our own way on the road. The automobile offers us a means to exercise direct control over our environment. When we enter the car we use it as an outlet for regaining a sense of control. Automobiles are powerful, and obedient. They respond instantly and gratifyingly to our command, giving us a sense of well being that comes with achieving control over one's environment.

The pace of life has increased for the majority of the population. Many have commented on the general feeling of loss of control in their lives. And yet it is human and natural to seek a sense of control in our lives, we want to feel we're getting somewhere, that we're not wasting time, that we're doing the right and just thing, that we're free to pursue our own interest—unfettered.

What happens when someone thwarts our sense of freedom? For example, while driving along in a pack of vehicles, a car in the left lane suddenly darts into your lane just ahead of you. Your foot automatically lifts from the gas pedal and taps the brakes, just enough to maintain distance. At this point, aggressive drivers feel thwarted because they were forced to alter what they were doing.

That driver forced you to lift your foot two inches. "What a moron. What an idiot." You feel an explosion of fury inside. It gets very hot. You might even begin to perspire. You grip the wheel harder. Now you've arrived at the decisive moment: you can let the emotion die out, or you can fan the flames with thoughts of indignation and retaliation. Aggressive drivers do not let the momentary emotional flare die down.

I discovered that many drivers I've worked with haven't learned the emotional skills they need to handle such routine emergency situations. The violation of their sense of personal freedom instantly arouses negative emotions that escalate in sequence from frustration to hostility to hatred. The fact is that aggressive driving is a cultural norm because our culture condones the expression of hostility whenever we feel wronged.[12]

If we are becoming a culture of road rage-aholics who do not have the emotional skills to control our anger impulses behind the wheel of a potentially lethal vehicle, this does not bode well for us making sustainable behavioral changes either for our health or in our personal relationships. Our road rage, and its accompanying sense of being disrespected or not valued, is not the only pervasive cultural behavior that elicits concern. Since the mid- to late 1980s, the level of celebrity worship in the United States has escalated to such a significant degree that tens of millions of Americans are obsessed with anything related to celebrity.

Both the escalation of road rage and the cultural phenomena of celebrity worship speak to us about what we *"are feeling deprived of from our psychological culture"*—our longing to be appreciated, to be respected and paid attention to. But instead, as Dr. Leon James says, we *"feel wronged"* by the environment we live in. In an increasingly competitive culture, rather than receiving recognition for our contributions, skills, or talents, we must work harder and *accomplish* more to fulfill the basic needs we have as human beings—to be valued by others, and to *belong*.

As with road rage, we can become triggered by our *reactive mind* when an external event provokes our internal stored pain or fear experience. Our *reactive mind* is largely responsible for why it is so difficult to make sustainable behavioral change—external stimuli activate pain or fear, and we self-soothe as a result. Behavioral Engagement re-informs our stored pain and fear experience, which then allows for successful, long-term behavioral change to occur.

Obsession with Celebrity

In his brilliant book *Fame Junkies*, Jake Halpern provides exhaustive research on the topic of our celebrity and fame obsessed culture. Halpern traveled across the country interviewing academic and health researchers who had studied the subject and provided insight into its origins.[13]

He grabs our attention from the opening chapter when he describes his hands-on experience of *going to fame school*. The opening sentence of this fascinating and disturbing book reads, *"Looking for aspiring celebrities in America is a little like looking for dehydrated nomads at a desert encampment—they are everywhere, and their thirst is so intense it's almost palpable."*

For the first seventy-five pages, Halpern describes the desperate lengths to which families will go to provide their child a chance at stardom and fame. The reader is mesmerized by the wrenching stories of longing and hope that these kids too will one day be famous like Paris Hilton—because when they are famous, the other kids at school, especially the ones who rejected or bullied them, will accept them. Then they can hang out with *the cool kids* at their school, and finally *belong*.

But children were not the only ones in Halpern's book longing for acceptance and recognition. He describes a very large population of adults who were either pursuing their own fame and celebrity or were so hungry for it that they found ways to bask in the *"reflected glory of celebrity"*—however remote or delusional it might be.

There are many ways these *thirsty nomads* find to have even the most glancing experience of fame. Depending upon the degree of longing, they may attempt to become celebrity personal assistants, which, as described in the book, are in reality *personal slaves* who devote their entire time, energy, and focus on doing whatever they are asked to do by their celebrity employer. They will go to any length to please, often at the expense of their own health and well-being.

Others become obsessed with a celebrity, sports team, or person of note so they too might bask in the "reflected glory" that the proximity to, or even the slightest association with, a celebrity can provide them. Halpern introduces the *Belongingness Theory*, developed by Roy F. Baumeister and Mark R. Leary at Case Western University in 1995, which suggests we have evolved over time a need for social acceptance. Halpern references psychologist Jaak Pankseep, of the Medical College of Ohio at Toledo, who claims that when we form social relationships, our brains produce opium-like chemicals that create feelings of pleasure.

Given the relationship–brain chemical interaction described here, one might logically question that if we have evolved a need for social relationships and are not successful at forming them—or the ones we have formed are not pleasure producing—can they drive us toward celebrity obsession? As we have previously learned, we want to move away from the pain of not belonging or of being rejected. We want to move toward the pleasure of social acceptance and being valued. If we associate ourselves in even the most remote way with a celebrity or a winning sports team, could this potentially fill an important need in our life?

The poignant ending to Halpern's book focuses on residents of The Fund, a home for frail, ill, or elderly show business retirees. It is not the description of their frailty or being forgotten that is haunting, but the persistent hope that they carry with them that before they die, *somehow* they can still achieve the recognition and admiration they longed for all their lives.

Other Considerations in Behavioral Change

The question about behavioral change has always been *"What exactly tips the scales in an individual's decision making to make a change in their life?"* Is it more information or cognitive awareness? Or is it the source of information from an authority figure, like a doctor's orders? Or is it something inside the person that produces behavioral change? Could it be all three of these or something more?

Too often a well-meaning health professional may want to force a change in a client's behavior and it simply cannot work. Rather it just brings even more resistance to change, as the client or patient feels entrapped in the facilitator's agenda. People may comply temporarily in a sort of codependent state, but sustainable change becomes elusive.

From a Behavioral Engagement perspective, people will make sustainable behavioral changes from a self-determination process that is based in retaining control over their choices; no one wants to be told what to do or how to do it. If individuals are persuaded to make changes that are directed from outside themselves, this will not *sustain* the changes—because no internal emotional process or shifts accompany the behavioral change, and that *emotional shifting* is a prerequisite for the highly desirable *sustained* behavioral change.

The Behavioral Engagement model achieves, by activating both *the thinking and feeling brains,* an interface with the full gamut of one's being—that of a whole person, physically, emotionally, socially, biochemically, environmentally, and spiritually. In doing so this interface evokes the *self-directed decision-making* process that has been shown to facilitate behavioral shifts and self-efficacy.

This extraordinary process can happen when the individual is invited to both remember and integrate, on conscious *and* unconscious levels, his or her innate self-knowledge and self-wisdom. True behavioral change can be successful and sustainable only when it evolves from an emotional process within the individual. Change must be nonthreatening and in alignment with the individual's values, beliefs, self-image, and finally, how the change will impact his relationship with others.

Over the Decades

There have been many theories and attempts to understand and define human behavior. As far back as 1796, medical science attempted to understand human behavior through a wide and often unorthodox variety of approaches and techniques. During that same year German physician Franz Joseph Gall developed phrenology, the study of formations or *bumps on the skull*, in an attempt to better understand human conduct through neurology rather than religion or philosophy. Since that time, many theories and therapies have evolved over the decades to address this most important component in how we live—how we behave.

The Theorists Workshop

One important "summit" of sorts was a special National Institute of Mental Health workshop, held in Washington, D.C., in 1991, titled the *Theorists Workshop.* It was conducted with the goal of identifying common elements between the various models of behavioral change for both understanding and being able to predict or modify human behavior.[14] The outcome of the *Theorists Workshop* resulted in the identification of eight key factors that were involved in the probability measurement of any given behavior.

These eight factors were identified as the potential conditions that determine behavior, as well as the keys for behavioral change:

> Intention toward the behavior—the person must have a strong and positive intention and commitment to making the change.

> Environmental limitations—it is important that there be no environmental factors that would prohibit or derail the behavioral change.

> Skill or ability to make the necessary changes—the person possesses the tools necessary, such as being able to read food labels or deal with language barriers.

> Anticipated outcomes for the behavioral change—the person has to hold the belief that the behavioral change will result in positive outcomes that will outweigh the disadvantages, such as time, cost, and inconvenience.

> Personal norms—the person receives more positive social feedback to perform the behavior than negative social feedback not to perform the behavior. Examples are stopping smoking and losing weight.

> Self-standards—performing the behavior is not in violation of the person's self-image or their values. For example, starting a diet that contains many unfamiliar foods may be socially awkward.

> Emotional response to behavioral changes—the emotional response and experience of the behavioral change has to be more positive than negative.

> Self-efficacy or self-determination—the person perceives that he or she is capable of performing the behavior and adapting the change to various circumstances or environments.

The workshop group identified the first three factors as *"necessary and sufficient"* to generate behavior change, and for behavior change to occur the person must have strong intentions, have the skills to do so, and not be restricted to accomplish the behavior change.

The remaining factors were identified as having an influence on the strength of the person's intention and a degree of influence on the outcomes. It was argued that unless an individual perceives a positive outcome for changing their behavior that is greater than the effort, time, and cost to make the change, that person will not have a strong motivation or intention to begin the behavioral change.

These factors appear in one form or another to be consistent throughout all behavioral change theories and approaches. What also appears to be consistent is the indication that unless you are in the category of being a *self-changer,* or a *self-directed* individual, there are considerable barriers and requirements for change to take place.

The Stages of Change model emphasizes this distinction in easy-to-understand language and identifies the various stages of consideration people are in related to whether or not they will initiate behavioral changes. The six stages of Prochaska's *Stages of Change model* include (1) pre-contemplation to change, (2) contemplation of making change, (3) preparation for making change, (4) taking action and making a change, (5) maintenance of that change, and (6) termination stage when the individual no longer needs to focus on or maintain the change they have made.

The self-changer appears to generally self-direct their intentions for change without requiring the same assistance as those who are not self-changers. Many self-changers have been able to stop smoking by just throwing their cigarettes away and never starting again or losing weight and not regaining it. They appear to move through the intention, evaluation, and action process more fluidly than others.

Self-changers or self-directed individuals seem to innately understand self-determined behavior. They use it without effort or prompting. Abraham Maslow's theory might identify such an individual as a person with high self-esteem who (1) possesses an innate ability to conduct a self-assessment, (2) has developed their own motivation and has resistance to triggers, (3) places him- or herself in an appropriate environment that supports and sustains their desired changes, and (4) has a high level of what appears to be a *critical component* to making behavioral change—*self-efficacy*—which is a belief that we can be in control of our destiny and live the life we envision or desire.

Developing Self-Efficacy

"People's beliefs about their capabilities produce designated levels of performance that exercise influence over events that affect their lives. Self-efficacy beliefs determine how people feel, think, motivate themselves and behave."

—Albert Bandura, PhD
Stanford University Professor, *Father of the Cognitive Theory*

Missing from the *Theorists Workshop* key factors or conditions is the mention of self-assessment or self-evaluation. People with high self-efficacy are resilient and self-directed individuals, who hold a belief that they can perform a desired task, accomplish goals, solve problems, and re-direct life events; they possess an innate mastery of their own behaviors. Most important, they are able to self-assess, learn from that assessment, and use what they learn to create the kind of change or shift they need to achieve their goals.

Unfortunately, what is required for many of us to arrive at the self-assessing process is a painful or frightening experience of such severity that we are willing to self-evaluate because of a pending threat to our *survival* on one of any number of levels. Is there another approach or alternative, instead of waiting for eminent threat to occur, that can facilitate us to self-assess and then make sustainable changes?

When behavior research is gathered on those who possess high self-efficacy, positive outcomes are greater for this group than for those of us who are not as self-directed. It is those of us who lack the innate self-efficacy skills who experience the frustrations, depression, and health-related issues that come from a sense of having little or no control over our lives and, as a result, a greater sense of hopelessness.

If we do not possess this innate self-efficacy, does this mean we are doomed to have little control over our lives or that our goals, dreams, and visions will not be realized? Are there interactions and tools that can facilitate or redefine our internal experiences to support greater self-efficacy? According to Professor Alberto Bandura of Cornell University, who pioneered research on self-efficacy, there are several ways an individual can develop it.

It can come from an inborn optimism or what he refers to as *constitutional resilience*. It can come from having mastery of a particular skill or task, and it can be acquired by observing someone who has been successful in reaching a goal or developing skills and modeling ourselves after them. He also says that self-efficacy can come from *verbal persuasion*. This is when we receive encouragement that is tied to our achievements, skills, knowledge, wisdom, or talents, rather than just empty praise for the sake of appeasement or flattery.[15]

A Remarkable Story

One of the most remarkable self-efficacy stories relates to a young man I met back in the mid-1970s, during my graduate school clinical internship in New York City. David came from a severely abusive family where he experienced both physical and emotional abuse from the time he was a child. David's mother had just separated from his father when she discovered she was pregnant with David, her second child, and she decidedly wanted to terminate the pregnancy.

Abortions were not legal at the time of his conception, but she tried to abort David numerous times through a variety of means. As a result David almost died at birth, but miraculously he survived. Because his parents did not divorce, he grew up hearing the story of how his unwanted birth trapped his mother in an unhappy marriage, and how she tried to *"get rid of him, but failed."*

Both the parents were verbally and physically abusive, but his father was also a rage-filled individual who, when triggered, often hit David. Once, the physical abuse was so severe that David had to be hospitalized. When the doctors questioned his mother about the marks on his body, she said he was fighting with his older brother. She told David that if he said anything to the doctors about what his father did, *she* would beat him.

A story like this does not usually end well. And yet this young man was a mature, self-assured, and highly self-directed individual. It puzzled a number of us at the clinic how David could experience such abuse and emotional wounding and still demonstrate self-efficacy. When his previous intern had graduated, I had the pleasure to get to know David, who was coming into the clinic for physical therapy because of a pulled hamstring he received while playing football.

In a casual conversation during one of his treatments, David shared his plans to earn a college degree in fitness, which was his passion. Aware that he came from a family that did not have the means, and possibly not the motive, to help him with his education, I asked David about his plans to pay for college. The answer he gave explained a lot. He said that throughout his schooling, as far back as he could remember, there were always teachers or other adults who believed he had the intelligence, talent, and personality to accomplish whatever he wanted to in life, and he now believed that as well.

Although David's parents physically and emotionally battered him, other adults respected and valued him. These *others* listened to him, acknowledged his abilities, and valued and celebrated the unique person he was. David said he was confident he could work his way through college and get his degree in an exercise-related major. And, he did. A number of years later, on a visit to New York, I ran into David and his wife. As planned, he had put himself through college, opened his own business, and become a successful personal trainer. David's upbringing was dysfunctional and abusive, but because others related to him with respect, compassion, and integrity, and treated him as a valued equal, he was provided a different emotional experience that cultivated his self-efficacy.

This is an unusual and extreme example of how the human spirit can rise above adversity. It also reinforces how the right environment can provide the nourishment for developing self-efficacy—which then enables us to create a positive and fulfilling life.

Enhancing Self-Efficacy with Relationship Dynamics

Is our self-efficacy enhanced when we receive a compassionate, nonjudgmental reflection of our worth and abilities? Do we expand the sense of what is possible for us to achieve when expectations and directives are removed from the interactions we experience with others? Our research with Behavioral Engagement has demonstrated that yes, we do. The Behavioral Engagement non-directive *Pure Presence* evidence-based tools are easy to learn, and can be applied to any and all situations where there is a desire to improve relationship dynamics. The tools and interactions are unlike other behavioral change methods.

These tools are not focused on or concerned with goals, outcomes, strategies, or statistics. In addition, there is no telling, advising, directing, recommending, or suggesting. Most important, there are *no expectations* of choices or outcomes. The application of the Behavioral Engagement tools within relationships produces a physical and psychological presence that provides the recipient an experience of being deeply valued, respected, and accepted as a unique individual.

This *Pure Presence* experience allows for greater self-discernment on both emotional and cognitive levels. *Pure presence* has demonstrated a belief-shifting ability that invites the recipient to take greater control over their life and behavioral choices. In essence, Behavioral Engagement can result in greater self-efficacy, even if that means the individual more confidently asserts *their desire not to change their behavior.*

This approach of honoring an individual's choice *not* to make a change in their behavior may seem counterintuitive to health professionals who believe it is in *the client's best interest* to make a change. However, as we have seen, even when an individual is presented with factual evidence that is counter to their beliefs, rather than considering making a change, *they dig their heels in more deeply* unless their feelings and beliefs are respected and honored.

What if the client innately creates a behavior that is his or her best survival strategy for this moment in time? Trying to force a change in that chosen adaptation could prove to be destructive. This honors Bandura's definition of self-efficacy states—that the individual possesses *"capabilities to produce designated levels of performance that exercise influence over events that affect their lives."* Choosing not to change at the moment can be a self-directed—and self-determined—choice for the highest good of the client. Respecting that choice can be transformational for both the recipient and the facilitator.

This dynamic is often seen when raising children. Parents' values are generally passed on to their children, yet often as the child becomes an adult, their behavior does not reflect those same values. The parents may feel their values are being rejected, and may want the grown-up child to change their behavior.

An example of this scenario is Michael, the son of a close family friend who has been attending a college his father thought was the right school for him to *"get ahead professionally."* After two years of studies, this very bright student decided he wanted to transfer to another college and take a certificate-of-study program in something he was passionate about.

Michael's father was upset about this decision, and the usual *"while you are living under my roof"* exchange began between father and son. There was tension, and angry behaviors were acted out as the conflict between the father's expectations for his son and the son's desire for autonomy escalated. Michael's mother applied Behavioral Engagement skills to the situation. She listened without judgment to both sides of the issue. She then shared with Michael's father that she felt Michael's decision to transfer schools was a choice he needed to be permitted to make. She also thought that because Michael felt so passionately about having some control over his life, it would be best for both parents to step back and let the son discern his options and choices.

The father, though clearly unhappy with the situation and not wanting his son to make some of the same mistakes he had made about his education, agreed to step back and allow their son to work though this decision. They would both support Michael's decision, whatever that turned out to be. This was a difficult choice for the father to make, as he felt he was doing the right thing for his son by insisting he not change schools. Although the father believed that his interceding in the son's decision to transfer was a way of *protecting* him rather than trying to *control* him, the parents let Michael know that both his mother *and* father would support whatever decision he made about his education. The subject was shelved. Then one evening, over dinner, Michael made an announcement.

He told his parents that he wanted to continue with his plans to do the certificate training program. However, he also realized that it would be best if he completed his college education and did not transfer, as doing so would result in him losing the course credits he had already earned and that his parents had paid for.

Michael said that knowing his feelings were respected and accepted, and that his family was willing to honor them, allowed him to better evaluate the situation from his parents' perspective rather than through the feelings of defensiveness he experienced when his ideas and plans were rejected. This is what allowed the *emotional shifting* to take place for Michael.

The Control Factor

Providing a pure, deeply respectful, egoless presence that is devoid of a personal or professional agenda removes the unconscious components that can sabotage positive outcomes. We often think we know what is best for others. We want to have that validated by having the other person accept and follow our advice. This interplay can be seen in many types of relationships, and to some extent we have grown used to this *codependent dynamic* as being a norm.

When this codependent element is replaced with authentic equality between individuals, along with the belief that people are capable of developing self-efficacy when the environment fosters it, what results is transformational outcomes—and healthy rather than unhealthy behaviors. Codependency is a real deterrent to fostering self-efficacy. At the institute where BE was developed, we believe that this is one of the major factors in today's health care culture that has led to the runaway health behaviors we saw in the previous chapter.

The current expert/patient hierarchy within health care promotes codependency in the same way the lack of a *patient-directed self-care* model does. In addition, we see an urgent need for demystified, whole-person health information that enables patients to have a greater understanding of and greater control over disease prevention, their health, and their well-being. *"You cannot change old behavior without new information."*[18] That new information needs to be understood and processed in a way that honors our emotions, beliefs, and values.

Fixing Medicine

Currently within medicine and health care delivery, *compliance* is the number-one issue with post-acute care, as well as chronic care. As referenced in Chapter 1, only one out of eight people will be able to shift their behaviors, even if their lives are at great risk and even though they wish to live long, healthy lives. There has been much discussion and examination of the role *intention* plays in people changing their behavior. What about the intention of the individuals who function as *facilitators* to behavioral change or desire to *enhance compliance* in others?

If intention is the number-one indicator of whether an individual is committed to taking action steps to change, then how important is it to address the influence of the intention of the individual who is *facilitating* behavioral change? The Behavioral Engagement model has identified that the intention of *both* individuals participating in the BE process is critical to the outcome of the interactions between them. An individual's intention is a powerful change agent. It can affect outcomes in a positive or a negative way.

From our pilot studies, as well as more than thirty years of internship and case studies data, we have *located* what we believe are several important missing elements for optimal behavioral change not found in current behavioral change models.[16] Behavioral Engagement *starts* with the *self-examination of the facilitator* and *an open acceptance of the client's intention.*

To focus only on the *recipient* of the process, and not the *individual facilitating the process*, is akin to doing couples counseling with only one of the couple partners present. To ensure the best possible outcome for both individuals, an understanding of *intention,* as well as an understanding of the *sacredness* of any interactive, is required. Please refer to Part 1, Chapter 2 for the comprehensive discussion on the subject.

As we come to the end of this *course* in transforming our relationships, I would like to invite you to review Part 1, Chapter 2, whenever you feel the need for a refresher course in the Behavioral Engagement model or if you would like a quick review on how to approach a potentially charged or challenging relational interaction.

I would love to hear about your experiences applying Behavioral Engagement with your family and friends. I also look forward to hearing your comments and answering any questions you may have about the model or about the research that was conducted on BE. Please feel free to e-mail me at changingbehaviorworkshops@gmail.com, and let me know how the Behavioral Engagement model has facilitated your relationships, both personal and professional.

Relationships are about BE-ing with others—not about DO-ing for them.
I hope that BE will allow you to BE with others in a new and joy-filled way!

Afterword

Congratulations on Completing the Behavioral Engagement Course

Congratulations on completing this tutorial and learning a new skill set for enhancing your relationship behavior and communication! Applying these tools and skills can assist you in many ways. Using them often and being patient with your process and development of the skills is worth the effort.

As you now understand *the big picture of behavior,* you can use this information not only to change the quality of your relationships but also to help others do so as well. If you are interested in *continuing your education* in Behavioral Engagement or becoming a *BE Communication Facilitator*, you can sign up for our 12 week training. Streamed videos, live tele-seminars, the BE Workbook, and relationship role playing sessions are all part of the training to deepen your understanding of Behavioral Engagement science and skills, and provide the opportunity to ask questions. If you would like more information about our trainings and one-day workshops in Behavioral Engagement, please visit us at www.changingbehavior.org or call 888-354-HEAL (4325).

About the Institute

The *course* you have just completed is derived from the Whole Health Education® program of the National Institute of Whole Health. The institute began in 1977, with the goal of addressing the *missing piece* in health care delivery. The idea behind creating the Whole Health programs was to provide health care practitioners continuing education courses that approached health and wellness from a Whole Person perspective rather than exclusively from the symptom-oriented treatment model they had been trained in.

As you might imagine, this was *radical thinking* back in 1977. The idea of Whole Person Health Care and empowering patients with demystified health information and health-behavior change skills was looked upon with raised eyebrows. In 1983, *Boston* magazine published an article about a workshop series NIWH faculty presented at the Boston Center for Adult Education. We had shockingly suggested that a person's health could be affected by the absence or presence of being loved and of being valued.

The article was quite unflattering about our presentation on a Whole Person health approach to preventing chronic disease, and suggested that we should not be allowed to teach such "unproven ideas". Now many decades later, NIWH is the national pioneer and leader of Whole Person Health and Whole Health Education—and integrative whole person focused medicine is everywhere. It appears NIWH was not too far off the mark in our teachings about Whole Person health and disease prevention!

Things have come a long way since 1977, but there is still much work to do in providing today's health care professionals with a new perspective on health and wholeness. NIWH is deeply grateful to be a contributor to the welcomed shift we see in health care today.

In 2005, the NIWH model became the mandate for "the practice of medicine in all settings." Both the Joint Commission on Accreditation of Health Care Organizations and hospitals and the Institute of Medicine identified these key guidelines:

- placing patients at the center of their health care decision making

- treating the patient as a whole person

- evidenced-based health education for prevention and disease management

Also of importance is that Medicaid/Medicare initiatives, currently voluntary but soon to be mandatory in 2013, include patient education, prevention of disease states, and "pay for performance" reimbursement guidelines for medical practices. "Pay for performance" reimbursements are based on a physician's documentation of patient education and other methods to address disease prevention outcomes.

In addition to the professional certification programs NIWH offers courses for nonprofessionals who would like to have Whole Health information for themselves, their families, or their community.

If you would like more information about our Whole Health Education professional training programs or wish to contact us about any of our Behavioral Engagement or Whole Health offerings please visit our sites at www.niwh.org or www.changingbehavior.org. You can also reach us by phone at 888-354-HEAL (4325).

Acknowledgments

It is only through the wisdom, support, and vision of many individuals that the model of whole-health education with Behavioral Engagement and Pure Presence was developed. This book is the result of much collaboration with these extraordinary individuals, and many decades of development and research. The early pioneers of whole health were the NIWH teachers and students, as well as the doctors and nurses who brought the model of whole-health education and Behavioral Engagement into their practices, medical centers, and hospitals to better serve their patients.

These visionary individuals wanted to practice more than symptom-oriented health care. What is quite remarkable is that they carried the vision of whole health with them at a time when the idea of self-directed health care was thought to be misguided, as patients *"did not have enough expertise to know what was best for them."* We all believed the opposite: that it was the *patients* and not the practitioners who were the real experts of their needs, that only the *patient* truly knew what was contributing to their illness, and that only they could keep themselves well.

There are many to thank. We start with Sherice and Timo Jacob, our editing, formatting, and layout team, whose assistance has made all the difference. Abundant thanks to Carol Arnold for years of support for this work. Heartfelt thanks to the brilliant Ken Zeno, PhD, *Changing Behavior*'s midwife.

Kudos and appreciation for the work of Mary-Anne Benedict, RN, MSN, for her unwavering support and tireless effort in assisting NIWH to better serve the nursing community. Very special thanks to my Nightingale Scholar mentor, Deva-Marie Beck, RN, PhD, and to my adviser and an NIWH advisory board member Barbara Dossey, PhD, RN. Profound thanks to you both for helping me achieve my dream of becoming a Florence Nightingale Scholar.

Sincerest thanks to our teachers and advisers, past and present: Lenny Goldberg; Cliff Whitehead, MA, MS; the Reverend David Hall; Linda Wells, PhD; Bill Croft, PhD; Mattie Cruz, MPH; Theresa Brimacombe, BA; Alan Gass, MD, FACC; Paul Bergeron, MD; Barry Sears, PhD; Laura Lubin, MSW, LICSW; Andrew Weiss, JA, MA; Joe Libonati, PhD; Mona Dorsinville, MD, MPH; Weifei Xei, OMD; Bernie Siegel, MD; Barry Sears, PhD; Walter Willett, MD, Dr PH; Anne Louise Gittleman, MS, PhD; Linda Bark, RN, PhD; Reggie Odom, MSW, CCP; John Reed, MD; Mona Lisa Schultz, MD, PhD; Maureen Spencer, RN, MSN; Elaine Carter, RN, BSN; Rebecca Shafir, MA, CCC; David Perlmutter, MD, FACN; Mark Hyman, MD; James Gordon, MD; Peter D'Adamo, ND; C. Norman Shealy, MD, PhD; Sherry Ryan, CHC, Rick Burkhardt, PhD; Jerry Kantor, MS, Lic. Acu., CCH; Barry Levine, MA; Susan Kilcoyne, BA; Daniel Dollar, BS, MLS; and Cela Doppelt, MD, FACOG.

Thanks to the many people who administratively and financially supported our research and development efforts, and the Boston-area hospitals, medical centers, and health care facilities where the program was presented, pilot-tested, and filmed: Ted Kaptchuck, OMD; Harvey Zarren, MD, FACC; Anna Seubert; Gail Mitton; Maureen Nuccitelli; Mary Grazen Brown; Clara Bowley; Kathleen Anderson; Linda Kenny; and Brian MacCormack. Enormous gratitude and thanks for our dedicated and passionate whole-health pilot studies interns and externs.

Many thanks to Massachusetts General Hospital; Harvard Medical School Center for Psychology and Social Change; Harvard Pilgrim Health Care: Women to Women co-founded by Christiane Northrup, MD; Cambridge Hospital Elder Care Services; Modern Assistance Medical Case Management Inc.; Addison-Gilbert Hospital; AtlantiCare Medical Center; the American Red Cross; Quincy Medical Center, an affiliate of Boston Medical Center; the Lemuel Shattuck Hospital; and St. Elizabeth's Hospital in Boston. These sites served as internship placements for hundreds of NIWH graduates. Lastly, special gratitude is extended to the thousands of pioneering NIWH students who, after graduating, went back to their health care environments and helped bring about many of the whole person care focused changes that we see today in mainstream medicine and health care.

References

Part I, Chapter One

1. Writer and explorer Dan Buettner has spent his life traveling the world. He is a writer for *National Geographic* who has combined his passion for travel with his love for exploring. He has traveled on a bicycle in Africa, Asia, South America, and more. His travels inspired him to write about societies with the longest life expectancy and the greatest happiness. His first book, *The Blue Zones: Lessons for Living Longer from the People Who've Lived the Longest,* was published in 2008 and became a best seller. His new book, *Thrive,* deals with the subject of happiness. http://www.npr.org/2010/11/28/131571885/how-to-thrive-dan-buettner-s-secrets-of-happiness

2. Thalamocortical neuron connections—http://www.ncbi.nlm.nih.gov/pmc/articles/PMC2277158/. "Fetal pain: a systematic multidisciplinary review of the evidence, Lee SJ, Ralston HJ, Drey EA, Partridge JC, Rosen MA, JAMA. 2005 Aug 24. Thalamocortical fibers begin appearing between 23 to 30 weeks' gestational age, while electroencephalography suggests the capacity for functional pain perception in preterm neonates probably does not exist before 29 or 30 weeks." http://www.ncbi.nlm.nih.gov/pubmed/16118385. Evidence about the capacity for fetal pain is limited but indicates that fetal perception of pain is unlikely before the third trimester. Little or no evidence addresses the effectiveness of direct fetal anesthetic or analgesic techniques.

3. Bentham, Jeremy; *Introduction to Principles of Morals and Legislation*; 1789; Moral Philosopher. Jeremy Bentham's classic *Principles* found pleasure and pain to be *"the sole motivators and the only absolutes in this world."* http://www.iep.utm.edu/bentham/. Freud's Pleasure Principle—in Freudian psychology, the pleasure principle is the psychoanalytic concept describing people seeking pleasure and avoiding suffering (pain) in order to satisfy their biological and psychological needs. http://en.wikipedia.org/wiki/Pleasure_principle

4. University of Michigan Study on Beliefs. Nyhan, Brendan, PhD; *"When Corrections Fail: The Persistence of Political Misconception,* originally published 2006; presented at the American Political Science Association; republished 2009. *"A new body of research out of the University of Michigan suggests that we base our opinions on our emotions, beliefs and world view and when presented with contradictory facts, we adhere even more strongly to our original beliefs, which are rooted in our emotions."* http://www.dartmouth.edu/~nyhan/nyhan-reifler.pdf

5. Beckman Institute for Advanced Science and Technology; Currently at University of Illinois, Urbana–Champaign; Cognitive Neuroscience; cognitive neuroscientists are researching and investigating emotional functioning—how interactions between various brain regions relate to mood and the link between the mental process of *knowing* and our emotions. http://www.beckman.illinois.edu/biointel/cns.aspx; http://www.msnbc.msn.com/id/11009379/ns/technology_and_science-science/t/political-bias-affects-brain-activity-study-finds

6. James-Lange Theory—*The* theory *says that "we experience emotion in response to physiological changes in our body. For example, we feel sad because we cry. Emotions are feelings resulting from physiological changes."* http://www.scienceforums.net/topic/3018-james-lange-theory-of-emotion/

7. Scherer, Klaus, 2007; *The Definition and Function of Emotions*; Social Science Information; September, 2007; 46–415. http://ssi.sagepub.com/content/46/3/415.extract. Scherer says that *"the principal design and function of emotion in humans is to mediate relationships. Events which are the focus of emotions are predominately social. They connect primarily with others; those with whom we have conflict; those with whom we are attached and those with whom we love."*

8. Stosney, Steven, PhD, April 8, 2011, *Psychology Today* Blog, *Why Couples Fight:* "[Cohabitating] couples don't fight about what they think they fight about. It's not 'the big [issues]' they identify in surveys: money, sex, kids, or house-work. Lovers fight

when they believe their partners don't care about how they feel. They fight about the pain of disconnection."
http://www.psychologytoday.com/blog/anger-in-the-age-entitlement/201104/marriage-problems-why-couples-fight

9. *Boston Globe,* November 19, 1996. A fifteen-year study by Harvard School of Public Health showed that up to 70% of all chronic disease is generated by lifestyles. *"The Harvard School of Public Health concluded on Nov. 19, 1996, after distilling virtually the entire body of research into cancer's causes, nearly 70 percent of cancer can be attributed to smoking, eating, and drinking habits and a sedentary lifestyle. Only 2 percent are traceable to environmental pollution and 10 percent to genetics. This report is an antidote for the fatalistic feelings people have that 'everything causes cancer.' Because there are no drawbacks or side effects from improving your diet and lifestyle, these changes should be made immediately, and to the greatest degree."*
http://www.drmcdougall.com/newsletter/nov_dec96.html

10. Kegan, Robert, PhD, Lisa Lahey, PhD, *Immunity to Change,* 2009; Harvard Business School Publishing Company; Introduction, page 1. *"Doctors can tell heart patients that they will literally die if they do not change their ways, and still only one in seven will be able to make the changes. They want to live out their lives, fulfill their dreams and watch their grandchildren grow up. These are not people who want to die. And, still they cannot make the changes they need in order to survive."*
http://www.uknow.gse.harvard.edu/leadership/LP3-4.html
http://www.leadershipeducators.org/Resources/Documents/Conferences/Spokane/allen.pdf

11. *Changing for Good;* "Stages of Change Model—A Six Stage Program for Overcoming Bad Habits and Moving Your Life Positively Forward." Harper Collins, 1994; James O. Prochaska, John O. Norcross, Carlo C. DiClemente—offers self-assessments to clarify each stage of change and how to make progress in each stage. Stages are identified as pre-contemplative, contemplative, preparation, action, maintenance, recycling, and termination.

12. The FHI.org international research organization, which manages health care and reproductive health research in more than seventy countries, tested the Stages of Change and published its behavioral change research outcomes in January 2002, and had this to say: *"As a psychological theory, the Stages of Change focus on the individual without assessing the role that structural and environmental issues may have on a person's ability to enact behavior change. In addition, since the Stages of Change present a descriptive rather than a causative explanation of behavior, the relationship between [the] stages is not always clear. Finally, each of the stages may not be suitable for characterizing every population."*

13. Obes Res. 2004 Sept; 12(9):1499–508. Longitudinal relationship between elapsed time in the action stages of change and weight loss. Logue EE, Jarjoura DG, Sutton KS, Smucker WD, Baughman KR, Capers CF. Source: Department of Family Practice, Summa Health System, 525 East Market Street, Suite 290, Akron, OH 44309-2090, USA. Discussion: The data support the concept of applying the Transtheoretical Model to the problem of managing obesity in primary care settings. The remaining challenge is to identify those factors that reliably move patients into the action and maintenance stages for long periods. http://www.ncbi.nlm.nih.gov/pubmed/15483215?dopt=Abstract ref: A September 2004 study at Summa Health System, tested the model on weight loss among patients. The outcome comments included, *"The data support the concept of applying the Transtheoretical Model to the problem of managing obesity in primary care settings. The remaining challenge is to identify those factors that reliably move patients into the action and maintenance stages for long periods."*

A follow-up article relating to the study by Weight Watchers Research offered this comment and observation: *"A two-year study of middle-aged overweight and obese men and women looked at the relationship between the Stages of Change for five weight-related behaviors; increased fruit and vegetable consumption, portion control, planned exercise, usual physical activity, or decreased dietary fat—and weight loss or gain. [The researchers] found that weight loss increased among those who spent more time in the action and maintenance stages for the five targeted behaviors. Proponents of using the Stages of Change model as a way to encourage behavior change believe that information and encouragement needs to be matched to a person's current stage. Finding ways to stay longer in the action and maintenance stages with fewer episodes in the relapse stage may prove to be an effective treatment for weight-loss plateaus. Unfortunately, there is limited research on how best to keep people in the preferred stages."*

14. In 2007, a large-scale Stages of Change study of 1,075 drug addicts seeking treatment for drug abuse in fifty-four treatment agencies in England was published. The study used structured interviews conducted during treatment intake. Data was collected on illicit drug use and other identified problems. The following outcomes were reported on the site PubMed.gov, U.S. National Library of Medicine, National Institutes of Health: *"FINDINGS: Results failed to support the hypothesis that taking steps should be associated with less frequent use of illicit opiates at follow-up. No statistically significant associations of any kind were found between readiness for change measures and use of opiates or stimulants at follow-up. CONCLUSIONS: Readiness for*

change measures were not associated with illicit drug use outcomes. Of the 12 hypothesized relationships between readiness for change measures and outcomes, our results show only one 'hit' and 11 'misses.'" http://www.ncbi.nlm.nih.gov/pubmed/17222285. http://onlinelibrary.wiley.com/doi/10.1111/j.1360-0443.2008.02439.x/full

15. *Changing for Good*; 1994; Harper; Chapter 1, page 21; J. Prochaska, PhD, J. Norcross, PhD, C. Diclemente, PhD. *"In fact, it can be argued that all change is self change. This [changing behavior] is tough work, but nothing else will do. For example, although many diets succeed in the short term, their long term success is quite low. Many dieters lose weight quickly, but six months after beginning a diet, many people weigh more than they did when they started."*

16. "A New Gauge to See What's Beyond Happiness; May 16, 2011; *New York Times*, Science section; by John Tierney; Martin E. P. Seligman, PhD, works on positive psychology, learned helplessness, depression, and on optimism and pessimism. He is currently Zellerbach Family Professor of Psychology and Director of the Positive Psychology Center at the University of Pennsylvania. He is well known in academic and clinical circles and is a best-selling author. His bibliography includes twenty books and 200 articles on motivation and personality. Among his better-known works are *Learned Optimism* (Knopf, 1991), *What You Can Change & What You Can't* (Knopf, 1993), *The Optimistic Child* (Houghton Mifflin, 1995), *Helplessness* (Freeman, 1975, 1993), and *Abnormal Psychology* (Norton, 1982, 1988, 1995, with David Rosenhan. http://www.ppc.sas.upenn.edu/bio.htm

Martin Seligman, PhD, the father of positive psychology, said that *"If we just wanted positive emotions, our species would have died out a long time ago. Why [do] couples go on having children even though the data clearly shows that parents are less happy than childless couples? Why [do] billionaires desperately seek more money even when there was nothing they wanted to do with it? We have children to pursue other elements of well-being. We want meaning in life. We want relationships."* http://www.nytimes.com/2011/05/17/science/17tierney.html?pagewanted=all

17. Comment: *"had been re-moralized with renewed interest in health and well-being."* Comments made by clinical director of the Pain and Stress Clinic at the Lemuel Shattuck Hospital, in Boston, about the outcomes and effect of Whole Health Educators™, using Behavioral Engagement model with both admitted patients and patients from the outpatient services clinic. "Our clinic at the Lemuel Shattuck Hospital was for poor and chronically ill patients who wanted to deal with refractory pain conditions. They were a difficult patient population. Between 1980 and 1989, each year we placed at least one or two interns from NESWHE [now the National Institute of Whole Health] to perform health education counseling with our clients. These interns were always well educated, sensitive, willing to work hard and able to re-moralize and spark renewed interest in health and well-being in our difficult patients. We came to rely on these placements because their enthusiasm for helping was a critical component of our clinical work to re-direct our patients towards a sense of self-help and self-reliance.

"On all levels, our relationships with NESWHE [now the National Institute of Whole Health] and its students was professional and of great value to our program." Ted Kaptchuk, OMD, former clinical director, Lemuel Shattuck Hospital Pain & Stress Relief Clinic, Jamaica Plain, MA.

18. The Golden Rule—The Golden Rule is endorsed by all the great world religions; Jesus, Hillel, and Confucius used it to summarize their ethical teachings. And for many centuries the idea has been influential among people of very diverse cultures. These facts suggest that the Golden Rule may be an important moral truth. The Golden Rule is best interpreted as saying, "Treat others only as you consent to being treated in the same situation." To apply it, imagine yourself on the receiving end of the action in the exact place of the other person (which includes having the other person's likes and dislikes). If you act in a given way toward another and yet are unwilling to be treated that way in the same circumstances, then you violate the rule. To apply the Golden Rule adequately, we need knowledge and imagination.

We need to *know* what effect our actions have on the lives of others. And we need to be able to *imagine* ourselves, vividly and accurately, in the other person's place on the receiving end of the action. With knowledge, imagination, and the Golden Rule, we can progress far in our moral thinking. The Golden Rule is best seen as a consistency principle. It doesn't replace regular moral norms. It isn't an infallible guide to which actions are right or wrong; it doesn't give all the answers. It prescribes consistency only so that our actions (toward another) are not out of harmony with our desires (in a reversed situation). It tests our moral coherence. If we violate the Golden Rule, then we're violating the spirit of fairness and concern that lie at the heart of morality. The Golden Rule, with roots in a wide range of world cultures, is well suited to be a standard that different cultures can appeal to in resolving conflicts. As the world becomes more and more a single interacting global community, the need for such a common standard becomes more urgent.

19. CARE Measure Survey; Mercer SW; Watt GCM; Maxwell M; Heaney DH. The development and preliminary validation of the Consultation and Relational Empathy (CARE) Measure: an empathy-based consultation process measure. *Fam Pract* 2004; 21(6): 699–705. The Consultation and Relational Empathy (CARE) Measure has been developed as a process measure of the consultation, based on a broad definition of *empathy*.http://fampra.oxfordjournals.org/content/22/3/328.full - ref-1 *Empathy* in this clinical context has been described as the ability to communicate an understanding of a patient's world and to act on that understanding in a therapeutic way. The aim of developing the CARE measure is to provide a tool for the evaluation of the quality of consultations in terms of the "human"aspects of medical care. By basing the measure on process rather than outcome, it provides doctors with direct feedback of their relational empathy, as perceived by their patients. For this reason, it has utility not only in research, but also as a tool for self-audit and has recently been accredited for use in GP appraisal and in Scotland.
http://www.npep.org.uk/
http://fampra.oxfordjournals.org/content/22/3/328.full

Part I, Chapter Two

1. The Consumer Federation of America reported that before the September 11, 2001, terrorist attack on the World Trade Center, many Americans did not consider financial planning as important as they did just one year after the terrorist attacks. What the event did was integrate what they had thought—*"financial planning is not that important"*—with what their feelings were after the terrorist attack— *"it feels important to be better financially prepared for unforeseen events that can affect my sense of security."* http://www.slideshare.net/Alfredh/financial-planning-now-more-important
This was originally reported by www.Americasaves.org.

2. Most waves of 8 Hz and higher frequencies are normal findings in the EEG of an awake adult. Waves with a frequency of 7 Hz or less often are classified as abnormal in awake adults, although they normally can be seen in children or in adults who are asleep. In certain situations, EEG waveforms of an appropriate frequency for age and state of alertness are considered abnormal because they occur at an inappropriate scalp location or demonstrate irregularities in rhythmicity or amplitude.
http://emedicine.medscape.com/article/1139332-overview

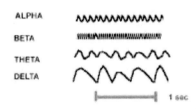

3. Harvard Faculty of Arts and Science Newsletter—*"Study Finds the Mind Is a Frequent but Not Happy Wanderer."* People spend 46.9 percent of their waking hours thinking about something other than what they're doing, and this mind wandering typically makes them unhappy. So says a study that used an iPhone Web app to gather 250,000 data points on subjects' thoughts, feelings, and actions as they went about their lives. The research, by psychologists Matthew A. Killingsworth and Daniel T. Gilbert of Harvard University, is described in the journal *Science.* "A human mind is a wandering mind; and a wandering mind is an unhappy mind," Killingsworth and Gilbert write. *"The ability to think about what is not happening is a cognitive achievement that comes at an emotional cost."* http://www.sciencemag.org/content/330/6006/932.abstract

4. Monitor Staff—*"Are young people more self-obsessed than ever before?"* by Sadie F. Dingfelder February 2011, Vol. 42, No. 2. "A narcissistic society would be a deeply lonely place," Barry says. According to some researchers, that is precisely where America is heading. Self-esteem is on the rise, with 80 percent of middle-school students scoring higher in self-esteem in 2006 than the average middle-school student in 1988, according to one study (in the *Review of General Psychology*, Vol. 14, No. 3). Among college students, subclinical levels of narcissism have steadily risen since the 1970s, other studies suggest. And though the diagnosis may be dropped from the *Diagnostic and Statistical Manual of Mental Disorders* (see Narcissism and the DSM), young people are much more likely than older adults to have ever experienced narcissistic personality disorder, according to a large-scale epidemiological study published in the *Journal of Clinical Psychiatry* (Vol. 67, No. 7).

5, 6. "The Eyes Are the Windows to the Soul"—Oxytocin as social brain; oxytocin increases gaze specifically toward the eye region of human faces. This may be one mechanism by which oxytocin enhances emotion recognition, interpersonal communication, and social approach behavior in humans. Findings suggest a possible role for oxytocin in the treatment of disorders characterized by eye-gaze avoidance and facial processing deficits. "It's said that the eyes are the window to the soul. They certainly are the window to the emotional brain. We know that the eye-to-eye communication—which is affected by oxytocin—is critical to intimate emotional communication for all kind of emotions—love, fear, trust, anxiety."

http://www.ncbi.nlm.nih.gov/pubmed/17888410

http://www.ncbi.nlm.nih.gov/pubmed/20047458

http://www.news-medical.net/news/2008/02/11/35124.aspx

7. Raymond George Hunt, applied psychologist and a former professor emeritus at the State University of New York, Buffalo, has said that there is *"quite a thin line that separates collaboration from manipulation."* Hunt is the author of numerous books, among them *Power and the Police Chief: An Institutional and Organizational Analysis (Studies in Crime, Law, and Criminal Justice)* and *Impacts of Racism on White Americans* by Raymond G. Hunt and Benjamin P. (Paul) Bowser: Mar. 26, 1996.

8. Institutes of Medicine, 2005—The Institute of Medicine reports that 90 million Americans suffer from poor health literacy, meaning that they cannot understand what they're being told about their health well enough to make good decisions about medications, appointments, consent forms, and treatments. According to the organization, "Poor health literacy has been associated with higher health care costs and with the growing disparities in U.S. health care."

http://sparkaction.org/content/mapping-paths-toward-health

http://www.ama-assn.org/ama/pub/about-ama/ama-foundation/our-programs/public-health/health-literacy-program/health-literacy-news.page.

9. NIWH, 2002—*"Creating a Renaissance of Relationship Centered Care"*—Reinvigorating Hospital and Medical Work Environments—Organization Values and Vision: "As the demands of each caregiver and support worker has increased, the work has become less meaningful and more tedious. This loss of meaning is one of the most important underlying reasons hospitals are having difficulty attracting and keeping sufficient workers ... they seek jobs separated into professional and occupational 'silos' that do not coordinate the work in the best interests of the patient." American Hospital Association Report 2002; "Foster Meaningful Work—*In Our Hands: How Hospital Leaders Can Build a Thriving Workforce."*

10. *Newsweek*, August 14, 2000; Howard Brody, MD, PhD, "Tapping the Power of Placebo"—Sugar pills are potent medicine when taken in the right spirit. Can we put them to practical use?"—"Virtually anything that sends a patient one of four messages—someone is listening to me; other people care about me; my symptoms are explainable; my symptoms are controllable—can bring measurable improvement in health." Brody teaches family practice and medical ethics at Michigan State University, East Lansing. He is the author of *The Placebo Response.* Also see February 26, 2001; Stephen Beruchka, MD; Professor, University of Washington's School of Public Health; article *"Is Our Society Making You Sick?"*—"America's health lags behind that of more egalitarian nations. Economic equality is the medicine we need. Does our focus on diseases, including risk factors and cures, stop Americans from looking at what would really keep us well?"

11. Yukio Ishizuka, MD—*The Surprising Reasons Couples Fight*—July 6, 2011, Bottom Line Publications Interview with Dr. Ishizuka, a Harvard-trained psychiatrist, who brings to his field several new questions: What is the objective of therapy? What does it mean to be well? How can we measure and improve well-being? During his more than thirty years of full-time clinical practice, he has developed and tested a paradigm of positive psychological health and a corresponding method of therapy to help people improve their sense of self, their intimate relationships, and their drive to achieve. He is the author of *Breakthrough Intimacy: Sad to Happy through Closeness.*

12. *"Leave your ego at the door."*—This quote is from Andrew Weiss, JD, MA, author of *Beginning Mindfulness.* Weiss was an instructor in Mindful Practice and Client Management for NIWH for more than ten years. He also served as the dean of students. Andrew Weiss is a longtime meditation student and teacher who is devoted to supporting his students to realize full awakening in each moment of their lives. He is deeply grounded in the Buddhist tradition and has added to that significant practice and study in the clairvoyant and Hindu traditions. To all of his teaching, he brings his fusion of mindfulness, Zen, devotional practice, and energy awareness. He has studied mindfulness meditation for many years in the United States, Europe, and Asia. His early studies of Zen focused on in the Korean tradition with Zen masters Seung Sahnh and Zen Master Su Bong. In 1989, he met the Vietnamese Zen monk Thich Nhat Hanh, and in 1991, he was ordained a brother in Thich Nhat Hanh's Order of Interbeing. In 1999, he was ordained by Zen priest Claude AnShin Thomas in the White Plum lineage of Japanese Soto Zen.

His study and practice in other, non-Buddhist traditions include, most significantly, his present studies with Sharon Turner in her Awakenings program.
http://www.beginningmindfulness.com/aboutandrew.html

Part II, Chapter Three

This chapter contains data and maps available from the U.S. Centers for Disease Control. Please note: The data shown in these maps were collected through the CDC's Behavioral Risk Factor Surveillance System (BRFSS). Each year, state health departments use standard procedures to collect data through a series of monthly telephone interviews with U.S. adults. Prevalence estimates generated for the maps may vary slightly from those generated for the states by the BRFSS as slightly different analytic methods are used.

1. CDC, 2010; U.S. Obesity Trends, Data and Statistics. The Centers for Disease Control provides the most current, up-to-date data on national obesity levels. A comprehensive report can be found at http://www.cdc.gov/obesity/data/trends.html.

2. Centers for Disease Control; "Obesity Trends among U.S. Adults." CDC's Behavioral Risk Factor Surveillance System 1991–2003; the statistics for these disorders are staggering and continues to grow each year. From 1991 through 2003 obesity in America went from an average of 11.9% to 23.5%, which represents a doubling of obesity rates in twelve years or a 1% increase each year. http://www.cdc.gov/obesity/data/trends.html

3. Centers for Disease Control; "Obesity Rates for Children in U.S. Ages 2–19," 2009; The following percentages are classified as overweight or obese, using the 95th percentile or higher of body mass index (BMI) values on the CDC growth chart. For non-Hispanic whites, 31.9% of males and 29.5% of females; for non-Hispanic blacks, 30.8% of males and 39.2% of females; for Mexican Americans, 40.8% of males and 39.5% of females. http://www.cdc.gov/obesity/data/trends.html

4. *Journal of the American Medical Association,* July 13, 2011; *"Harvard Professor Under Fire After Calling for Obese Children to Be Removed from Homes in Severe Cases"*—"Harvard University Professor Dr. David Ludwig is under attack for his public call this week for some obese children to be taken from their parents to protect their health. Ludwig stated that '[i]n severe instances of childhood obesity, removal from the home may be justifiable, from a legal standpoint, because of imminent health risks and the parents' chronic failure to address medical problems.' That legal standpoint may need a bit more work. Ludwig is an obesity expert at Children's Hospital Boston and associate professor at the Harvard School of Public Health. His comments came in the *Journal of the American Medical Association*."
http://www.uslaw.com/library/Legal_Commentary/Harvard_Professor_Under_Fire_Calling_Obese_Children_Removed_Homes _Seve.php?item=1108723 4.B—"Fat Penalty"—Fat Fines and Higher Insurance Fees; April 7, 2011; The 30 pound club at www.drchet.com.

"The governor of Arizona and many companies in the U.S. are proposing penalizing people who are overweight by charging them more for healthcare. Governor Brewer wants to charge Medicaid patients $50 per year if they don't work with a physician to meet healthcare and weight loss goals. Companies are doing the same—if they hire you in the first place. Health insurance companies charge more for health insurance—if they will cover you in the first place. Is this approach fair?"

5. Alcohol and Behavior—In the United States, in 2009, 59% of all death for adults older than twenty-five years of age are related to six categories of health-risk behaviors that resulted in cardiovascular or cancer deaths: (1) tobacco use (2) alcohol and other drug use; (3) sexual behaviors that contribute to STDs, including human immunodeficiency virus (HIV) infection as well as unwanted pregnancy; (4) unhealthy dietary behaviors; (5) physical inactivity; (6) behaviors that contribute to unintentional injuries or violence. Health-risk behavior studies developed by the CDC identify these behaviors as being frequently interrelated and established during childhood and adolescence. These behaviors then extend into adulthood. http://www.cdc.gov/mmwr/preview/mmwrhtml/ss5905a1.htm. http://www.cdc.gov/yrbs.

6, 7. Tobacco Use; American Council for Drug Education; In 2010, the use of tobacco and smoking still remained the leading preventable cause of disease, disability, and death in the United States. Between 1964 and 2004, cigarette smoking caused an estimated 12 million deaths, including 4.1 million deaths from cancer and 5.5 million deaths from cardiovascular diseases. http://www.acde.org/common/Tobacco.htm

7. Tobacco-Related Cancers; Appendix III; International Comparable Prevalence Estimates; Appendix III provides adjusted and age standardized data on the prevalence of tobacco use for the 135 member states that provided data that satisfied criteria

outlined in the Technical Note section. The adjusted estimates are more important for individual countries, since the total number of smokers in each country can be obtained using these estimates. Technical Note I
http://www.who.int/tobacco/mpower/mpower_report_prevalence_data_2008.pdf
http://www.cancer.org/acs/groups/content/@epidemiologysurveilance/documents/document/acspc-026238.pdf
http://www.cdc.gov/nchs/data/series/sr_10/sr10_249.pdf - smoking; pg 96 Table 25

8, 9, 10. Use of Alcohol; Binge Drinking; Long-Term Use of Alcohol; Published by the Centers for Disease Control: Alcohol is one of the most widely used drug substances in the world. Alcohol use and binge drinking among Americans is a serious health problem. Binge drinking is defined as four or more drinks within one to several hours for women and five or more drinks within one to several hours for men. Fifty-two percent of adults aged eighteen and up are current, regular drinkers. The CDC in their Alcohol Fact Sheet lists the risks of binge drinking and its potential outcomes.
http://www.cdc.gov/alcohol/fact-sheets/alcohol-use.htm *Alcohol-Related Disease Impact (ARDI)*. Atlanta, GA: CDC. Available at http://www.cdc.gov/alcohol/ardi.htm. March 28, 2008;
http://www.cdc.gov/nchs/data/series/sr_10/sr10_249.pdf alcohol pg 19; tables 26–27 pgs 98–99.

11, 12. Drug Use; National Institute on Drug Abuse; "Illicit drug use in the United States has risen to its highest level in eight years, according to the 2009 National Survey on drug use and health. Last year, 8.7 percent of Americans aged twelve years and older—an estimated 21.8 million people—said they used illicit drugs in the month prior to the survey, which represents a 9 percent increase over the 2008 survey. The increase was particularly high among twelve to seventeen year olds and young adults aged eighteen to twenty-five."
http://www.nida.nih.gov/NIDA_notes/NNvol23N3/tearoff.html

The annual NSDUH survey is sponsored by SAMHSA. The 2009 results are based on responses from 68,700 civilians nationwide who do not live in institutions. The report is available online at www.oas.samhsa.gov/NSDUH/2k9NSDUH/2k9Results.htm Source: Substance Abuse and Mental Health Services Administration, 2010. *Results from the 2009 National Survey on Drug Use and Health: Volume I. Summary of National Findings* (Office of Applied Studies, NSDUH Series H-38A, HHS Publication No. SMA 10-4586). Rockville, MD. [Full Text]; http://www.usnodrugs.com/drug-addiction-statistics.htm

13, 14. Intimate Partner Violence and the Impact of the Economy on Domestic Violence; CDC Report; "IPV resulted in 2,340 deaths in 2007. Of these deaths, 70% were females and 30% were males. The medical care, mental health services, and lost productivity (e.g., time away from work) cost of IPV was an estimated $5.8 billion in 1995. Updated to 2003 dollars, that's more than $8.3 billion." http://www.cdc.gov/violenceprevention/pdf/IPV_factsheet-a.pdf
A report by the national Network to End Domestic Violence (NNEDM) identifies the influence of economical stress and DPV: http://dvam.vawnet.org/docs/materials/09-resource-packet/Issue_FactsSheets_Handouts/ImpactofEconomy_FactSheet.pdf

15, 16. The Emotional and Physical Abuse of Children; "Children are suffering from a hidden epidemic of child abuse and neglect. Over 3 million reports of child abuse are made every year in the United States; however, those reports can include multiple children. In 2009, approximately 3.3 million child abuse reports and allegations were made involving an estimated 6 million children." http://www.childwelfare.gov/pubs/factsheets/long_term_consequences.cfm

These children were neglected or abused by their parents 81.1% of the time and by their extended families 6.5% of the time. Women abused children more frequently than men did, with the *child's biological mother* being the most frequent abuser. The secondary effects of child abuse results in elevated rates of criminal behavior. U.S. government statistics show that 14% of all men in prison were reported to have been abused as children, and 36% of all women in prison were abused. In addition, children who experience child abuse and neglect are 59% more likely to be arrested as a juvenile, 28% more likely to be arrested as an adult, and 30% more likely to commit violent crime.
http://www.acf.hhs.gov/programs/cb/pubs/cm08/cm08.pdf
http://www.childwelfare.gov/pubs/factsheets/long_term_consequences.cfm
http://www.acf.hhs.gov/programs/cb
http://www.childhelp.org/pages/statistics

17. Gambling; Research reveals that in America, approximately 2.5 million adults suffer from compulsive gambling, about 3 million are considered problem gamblers, around 15 million adults are under the risk of becoming problem gamblers, and 148 million fall under the low-risk gambler category.
http://rehab-international.org/gambling-addiction/gambling-addiction-statistics

18. Compulsive Shopping; Lorrin Koran, MD, researcher at Stanford University, in 2006 published a study in the *American*

Journal of Psychiatry, by Koran and his colleagues, with more than 2,500 subjects. They study concluded that compulsive overspending or overshopping affects approximately 6% of the U.S. population, or 17 million people, with equal amounts of men and women. Other surveys estimate 2%–12%. http://ajp.psychiatryonline.org/cgi/content/abstract/163/10/1806

19. Hoarding; More than 6 million people, or one out of twenty, in the United States hoard. It is calculated that "2%–5% of Americans may meet the criteria for being hoarders," says David Tolin, PhD, a hoarding expert and author of *Buried in Treasures.* http://www.webmd.com/mental-health/features/harmless-pack-rat-or-compulsive-hoarder?page=2

20. Nonsuicidal Injurious Behavior; Research addressing the epidemiology and phenomenology of nonsuicidal self-injury (NSSI) among adolescents in articles on Medline and Psychinfo indicate a lifetime prevalence of NSSI ranging from 13.0% to 23.2%. Reasons for engaging in NSSI: to regulate emotions and to elicit attention. http://www.ncbi.nlm.nih.gov/pubmed/17453692/

21. Infidelity—According to research by Davis Bush and Todd Shackleford at the University of Texas, 30% to 60% of all married individuals in the United States will engage in infidelity behaviors sometime during their marriage.
http://homepage.psy.utexas.edu/homepage/Group/BussLAB/pdffiles/susceptibility_to_infidelity-jrp-1997.pdf
http://homepage.psy.utexas.edu/homepage/Group/BussLAB/pdffiles/susceptibility%20to%20infidelity-jrp-1997.pdf

Part II, Chapter Four

1. "Harvard Mastery of Stress Study"; J Behav Med: 1997 Feb; 20 (1):1–13. "Feelings of parental caring predict health status in midlife: a 35-year follow-up of the Harvard Mastery of Stress Study"; Russek LG, Schwartz GE. Source: Harvard University Student Health Service, Cambridge, Massachusetts, USA. Abstract: In the early 1950s, multiple-choice scores reflecting feelings of warmth and closeness with parents were obtained from a sample of healthy, undergraduate Harvard men who participated in the Harvard Mastery of Stress Study. Thirty-five years later, detailed medical and psychological histories and medical records were obtained. Ninety-one percent of participants who did not perceive themselves to have had a warm relationship with their mothers (assessed during college) had diagnosed diseases in midlife (including coronary artery disease, hypertension, duodenal ulcer, and alcoholism), as compared to 45% of participants who perceived themselves to have had a warm relationship with their mothers. A similar association between perceived warmth and closeness and future illness was obtained for fathers. Since parents are usually the most meaningful source of social support in early life, the perception of parental love and caring may have important effects on biological and psychological health and illness throughout life. PMID:9058175 [PubMed—indexed for MEDLINE] http://www.ncbi.nlm.nih.gov/pubmed/9058175

2. Harvard Mastery of Stress Study revisited by Linda Russek, PhD, and Gary E. Schwartz, PhD,
 director of the VERITAS Research Program, is a professor of psychology, medicine, neurology, psychiatry, and surgery at the University of Arizona and director of its Laboratory for Advances in Consciousness and Health and its Center for Frontier Medicine in Biofield Science. After receiving his doctorate from Harvard University, he served as a professor of psychology and psychiatry at Yale University, director of the Yale Psychophysiology Center, and co-director of the Yale Behavioral Medicine Clinic. Schwartz has published more than 400 scientific papers, edited eleven academic books, and is the co-author of *The Living Energy Universe.* http://veritas.arizona.edu/
Linda Russek, PhD, is the president of the Family Love and Health Foundation. For twenty years she was the research psychologist at the Harvard University Health Services and director of the Harvard Mastery of Stress Follow-Up Study.
http://www.psychosomaticmedicine.org/content/59/2/144.full.pdf

3, 4. Susan A. Everson, PhD, MPH—widely published researcher relating to areas of health and hopelessness. An epidemiologist at the Western Consortium for Public Health in Berkeley, California, she and her colleagues, including epidemiologist George A. Kaplan of the California Department of Health Services in Berkeley, co-authors of a hopelessness study, say that *"It looks like people who experience a pervasive sense of hopelessness are at increased risk for a variety of serious health problem."*

Studies: http://www.psychosomaticmedicine.org/content/58/2/113.full.pdf
http://www.sciencenews.org/pages/pdfs/data/1996/149-15/14915-05.pdf
http://findarticles.com/p/articles/mi_m1200/is_n15_v149/ai_18205252/
Michael F. Scheier, a psychologist at Carnegie Mellon University in Pittsburgh, says, "Much previous research indicates that optimism in the face of losses and failures promotes mental and physical health, whereas pessimism does the reverse." http://www.thefreelibrary.com/Hopelessness+tied+to+heart,+cancer+deaths.-a018205252

5. June 25, 1997, *Journal of the American Medical Association*, (SN: 6/21/97, p. 381). Also, June 25, 1997; *LA Times* medical writer Terence Monmaney; "Friends are nothing to Sneeze at, Researchers Say." "Probing the ever elusive mind-body

connection, a new study of 276 people who got purified cold viruses sprayed up their noses has reached a conclusion that is nothing to sneeze at: Loners were four times more likely to come down with a cold than people rich in relationships. The study strengthens the popular but difficult to prove notion that an active network of family, friends, neighbors and even co-workers can bolster one's resistance to disease, perhaps by activating the immune system."
http://articles.latimes.com/1997-06-25/news/mn-6646_1_social-support

6. "Pet Ownership, but Not ACE Inhibitor Therapy, Blunts Home Blood Pressure Responses to Mental Stress"; *Journal of the American Heart Association*; Hypertension. 2001; 38: 815–820; Karen Allen, Barbara E. Shykoff, Joseph L. Izzo Jr.—Study by Karen Allen, PhD and colleagues. Allen, a researcher at the State University of New York at Buffalo, found that stockbrokers with hypertension who adopted a cat or dog had lower blood pressure readings in stressful situations than did their non-pet-owning counterparts. http://hyper.ahajournals.org/content/38/4/815.full
http://scienceblog.com/community/older/1999/A/199900345.html

7. Dr. Ellen Langer is a professor in the psychology department at Harvard University. Her books written for general and academic readers include *Mindfulness, The Power of Mindful Learning, On Becoming an Artist*, and *Counterclockwise*. Langer has described her work on the illusion of control, aging, decision making, and mindfulness theory in more than 200 research articles and six academic books. Her work has led to numerous academic honors, including a Guggenheim Fellowship, the Award for Distinguished Contributions to Psychology in the Public Interest of the American Psychological Association, the Distinguished Contributions of Basic Science to Applied Psychology award from the American Association of Applied & Preventive Psychology, the Adult Development and Aging Distinguished Research Achievement Award from the American Psychological Association, the James McKeen Cattel Award, and the Gordon Allport Intergroup Relations Prize.
http://www.ellenlanger.com/information/9/read-chapter-one-of-counterclockwise

8, 9. "Satisfaction with Life Scale," *Journal of Personality Assessment*, 1985, *49*, 1 Ed Diener, Robert A. Emmons, Randy J. Lar.sem and Sharon Griffin. University of Illinois at Urbana–Champaign "Abstract: This article reports the development and validation of a scale to measure global life satisfaction, *The Satisfaction with Life Scale (SWLS)*. Among the various components of subjective well-being, the SWLS is narrowly focused to assess global life satisfaction and does not tap related constructs such as positive affect or loneliness. The SWLS is shown to have favorable psychometric properties; including high internal consistency and high temporal reliability. Scores on the SWLS correlate moderate to high with other measures of subjective well-being, and correlate predictably with specific personality characteristics. It is noted that the SW~1Ss suited for use with different age groups, and other potential uses of the scale are discussed."

Lifestyles of the Rich and Famous was a television series that aired in syndication from March 31, 1984, to September 2, 1995. The show featured the extravagant lifestyles of wealthy entertainers, athletes, and business moguls. It was hosted by Robin Leach for the majority of its run. When Leach was joined by Shari Belafonte in 1994, the show was renamed *Lifestyles with Robin Leach and Shari Belafonte*. Leach ended each episode with a wish for his viewers that became his signature phrase: *"champagne wishes and caviar dreams."* http://en.wikipedia.org/wiki/Lifestyles_of_the_Rich_and_Famous

10. "Higher income improves life rating but not emotional well-being." PhysOrg.com. 7 September 2010. Princeton University professors Angus Deaton, the Dwight D. Eisenhower Professor of International Affairs and Professor of Economics and International Affairs, and Daniel Kahneman, the Eugene Higgins Professor of Psychology and Professor of Psychology and Public Affairs (Emeritus), analyzed more than 450,000 life evaluation survey responses of randomly selected U.S. residents:

"We conclude that lack of money, less than $75,000 income, brings both emotional misery and low life evaluation; similar results were found for anger," write the authors in the report. "Beyond $75,000 in the contemporary United States, however, higher income is neither the road to experienced happiness nor the road to the relief of unhappiness or stress, although higher income continues to improve an individual's life evaluations." http://www.physorg.com/news203060471.html
http://www.physorg.com/news203060471.html. Retrieved 20 September 2010.

11. *Journal of Personality and Social Psychology* 2011 American Psychological Association; 2011, Vol. 101, No. 1, 164–184 0022-3514 DOI: 10.1037/a0023663;"What Is More Important for National Well-Being: Money or Autonomy?; A Meta-Analysis of Well-Being; Burnout; and Anxiety across 63 Societies"; Ronald Fischer and Diana Boer. Victoria University of Wellington.
http://www.apa.org/pubs/journals/releases/psp-101-1-164.pdf

12. In his congressional testimony to the Subcommittee on Surface Transportation and Infrastructure, U.S. House of Representatives (Washington, D.C.), July 17, 1997, Dr. Leon James, professor of traffic psychology, University of Hawaii, Honolulu, said, *"Road rage is a culturally acquired [behavior]. Road rage is becoming a major problem for motorists and high*

mileage company car drivers. Seventy-eight percent of company car drivers said that at some time another driver had verbally abused them, while 21% said that another driver had forced them to pull over or off the road. However, although most cases of road rage did not lead to physical injury—only 3% suffered from physical violence—10% suffered damage to their car from road ragers.

"[The combination of]Driving and habitual road rage has become virtually inseparable."
http://www.drdriving.org/articles/testimony.htm

13. *Fame Junkies—the Hidden Truth behind America's Favorite Addiction*; Jake Halpern; Houghton Mifflin Company, 2007, Boston. "Why do more people watch *American Idol* than the nightly news? What is it about Paris Hilton's dating life that lures us? Why do teenage girls when given the option of 'pressing a magic button' and become stronger; smarter; famous; or more beautiful, predominately opt for fame? *Fame Junkies* reveals how psychology, technology, and even evolution conspire to make the world of red carpets and velvet ropes so enthralling to all of us on the outside looking in."
http://www.jakehalpern.com/famesurvey.php

14. Fishbein, M. et al. *"Factors influencing behavior and behavior change."* Final report prepared for NIMH Theorists Workshop. Washington, D.C., 1991; A special National Institute of Mental Health workshop titled the *Theorists Workshop* was held with a goal of identifying common elements between the various models of behavior change for both understanding and being able to predict or modify human behavior. The outcome of the *Theorists Workshop* resulted in the identification of eight key factors that were involved in the probability measurement of any given behavior.
These eight factors were identified as the potential conditions that determine behavior, as well as the keys for behavioral change. http://www.technologyreview.com/biomedicine/25693/

15. *Holist Nurs Pract.;* 2005 Mar–Apr; 19(2): 74–7 *Improving Healthcare Delivery with the transformational whole person care model*; Donadio G; [NIWH] The New England School of Whole Health Education, Wellesley, MA 02482, USA—A Whole Person Care model was developed by [NIWH] The New England School of Whole Health Education following a two-year pilot study that demonstrated the transformational effects of Whole Health Education®.
This holistic model of health education and behavioral interaction provides a tool for nurses, physicians, and staff to redirect the momentum of care toward in-the-moment, relationship-centered whole person care, improving healthcare worker and patient satisfaction and outcomes. PMID: 15871590 [PubMed - indexed for MEDLINE]
NIWH List of Pilots Links:
http://www.ncbi.nlm.nih.gov/pubmed?term=Holist%20Nurs%20Pract%3B%202005%20Mar-Apr%3B19(2)%3A%2074-7%20Improving%20Healthcare%20Delivery
http://www.wholehealtheducation.com/lemuel-shattuck-hospital/
http://www.wholehealtheducation.com/pilot-trial-whole-health/
http://www.wholehealtheducation.com/whole-health-healthcare-model/
http://www.wholehealtheducation.com/2011/03/holistic-nursing/
http://www.wholehealtheducation.com/2011/05/marinamedical/
http://www.prlog.org/11670210-healthcorps-army-seeks-to-advance-advocacy-efforts-with-whole-health-education.html

15. Alberto Bandura, PhD, Emory University professor; 1994. Self-efficacy; In V. S. Ramachaudran (Ed.); *Encyclopedia of Human Behavior;* (Vol. 4, pp. 71–81. New York: Academic Press. Reprinted in H. Friedman [Ed.]; *Encyclopedia of Mental Health*. San Diego: Academic Press, 1998). According to Professor Alberto Bandura, of Cornell University, who pioneered research on self-efficacy, there are several ways an individual can develop self-efficacy. It can come from an inborn optimism or what he refers to as *constitutional resilience*, it can come from having mastery of a particular skill or task, and it can be acquired by observing and someone who has been successful in reaching a goal or skills and modeling ourselves after them. He also says that self-efficacy can come from *verbal persuasion*. This is when we receive encouragement that is tied to our achievements, skills, knowledge, wisdom, or talents, rather than just empty praise for the sake of appeasement or flattery.
http://des.emory.edu/mfp/self-efficacy.html

16. Quote: "You cannot change old behavior without new information." Quote attributed to Georgianna Donadio, founder of the Behavioral Engagement and the National Institute of Whole Health. This quote relates to the NIWH Behavioral Engagement™ model developed over thirty-five years. The Behavioral Engagement model addresses the science of behavioral change. Part of the construct of the model is the integration of what is identified as "alpha and beta brain overlap," which produces new, integrative information, perspective, and awareness in the individual who experiences Behavioral Engagement and its *Pure Presence* component.
http://www.wholehealtheducation.com/whole-health-education-pilot-studies/

CPSIA information can be obtained at www.ICGtesting.com
Printed in the USA
BVOW03s2253110716

455147BV00019BA/108/P